Church and State in Confrontation

A Sociological Study of

Church-State Relations from

Old Testament Times to the Present

By the Author:

Bureaucracy in Higher Education
Community Welfare Organization
The Jehovah's Witnesses
Social Work: An Introduction to the Field
A Symphony of Prayer (Editor)
Toward a Philosophy of Organized Student Activities

HERBERT STROUP is Professor of Sociology and Dean of Students at Brooklyn College of the City of New York, where, since 1942, he has held every teaching rank. He was graduated from Union Theological Seminary and holds a D.Soc.Sc. degree from the Graduate Faculty of The New School for Social Research.

Dean Stroup is a member of the executive committee for Church World Service and Fellow of the National Council on Religion and Higher Education.

His previous books include *The Jehovah's Witnesses, Social Work: An Introduction to the Field, Community Welfare Organization, Toward a Philosophy of Organized Student Activities,* and *Bureaucracy in Higher Education.*

Church and State
in Confrontation

HERBERT Hewitt STROUP

The Seabury Press

NEW YORK

92913

ACKNOWLEDGMENTS

Grateful acknowledgment is made to the following authors and publishers for permission to use copyrighted material, quoted at length, from
the titles listed:

American Academy of Arts and Sciences—Langdon Gilkey, "Social and
Intellectual Sources of Contemporary Protestant Theology in America,"
and Franklin H. Littell, "The Churches and the Body Politic," in
Daedalus, Winter, 1967.

Doubleday & Company—Franklin H. Littell, *From State Church to
Pluralism,* copyright © 1962 by the author, reprinted by permission
of the publisher.

Harper & Row, Publishers—James M. Gustafson, *Treasure in Earthen
Vessels: The Church as a Human Community,* copyright © 1961 by the
author, reprinted by permission of the publisher; and G. van Der Leeuw,
Religion in Essence and Manifestation (Tourchbook), Volume I (Eng.
ed. pub. by George Allen & Unwin, Ltd.).

Holt, Rinehart & Winston—Thomas Ford Hoult, *The Sociology of Religion,* copyright © 1958 by the publisher.

The Macmillan Company—Harvey Cox, *The Secular City: Secularization
and Urbanization in Theological Perspective,* copyright © 1965 by the
author.

To My Parents
Margaret Hewitt Stroup
William Valentine Stroup

"Lord, with what care Thou hast begirt us round!
Parents first season us. . . ."

George Herbert (1593-1633)

Preface

The subject of this book is one which in the past decade or more has come to the forefront of interest and concern among Americans of diverse religious convictions and associations. The literature on the subject of church and state relations increases by leaps and bounds from year to year, although the resulting popular achievement of consensus, significant as it is on certain matters, fails to keep pace. This book does not seek to "solve" the problems of church and state relations, but aims simply to lay before the general reader some of the issues and some of the knowledge which has been developed about these issues. The references employed throughout the book will provide the general reader with leads to further exploration of an exceedingly complex and important subject.

My own background as a sociologist has contributed, as will be perceived, to the way in which church and state relations are conceived. But several concrete opportunities also have greatly sharpened my interest and thinking. One was the preparation of a paper entitled "The Welfare State" for the annual meeting of the Board of Managers of Church World Service held in February, 1963, at Atlantic City, New Jersey. I am deeply indebted to my colleagues on the board (now known as Church World Service Department of the Division of Overseas Ministries of the National Council of the Churches of Christ in the United States of America) for their constant encouragement. Mr. James MacCracken, Executive Director of Church World Service and Associate Secretary of the Division of Overseas Ministries, and other members of his staff have regularly provided me with helpful stimulation on the subject.

Also, I was enriched by being a member of the Commission on Church and State of the Council for Christian
Social Action of the United Church of Christ. To the
members of the commission, and to Ray Gibbons particularly, I wish to express heartfelt appreciation. Through
this membership I was given another opportunity to write
on the subject.[1]

I also wish to acknowledge the helpfulness of being a
participant and leader in the National Study Conference
on Church and State, held at Columbus, Ohio, in February, 1964, under the sponsorship of the Department of
Religious Liberty of the National Council of the Churches
of Christ in the United States of America. Dean M. Kelley
and others associated with the conference greatly increased
my understanding of the subject.

Mr. Barry Josephson, formerly a Fellow in the Department of Student Services of Brooklyn College, skillfully
checked all of the quotations and references for accuracy.

Also, I am deeply indebted to my colleagues in the
Department of Student Services for their devotion to duty,
and especially to the units heads without whom these
pages never would have been written: Roberta Baker,
Myron Berrick, Richard Fitzpatrick, Ernst Koch, Archie
McGregor, Samuel Pearlman, Mary Stapleton, and Shirley
Wedeen.

Trudi Stroup, my daughter, helped greatly in the preparation of this book, including the task of preparing the
indexes. Susan Scott also helped.

Of course, in no way is any individual or organization
responsible for the declarations and shortcomings of this
book. The book does not represent the official position of
any other individual or organization.

Contents

ix

Contents

Church and State in Confrontation

I

The Problem of
Church-State Relationships

DIVERSITY

The singular fact of disestablishment in American history has shaped a distinctive, though complex, set of circumstances surrounding the interrelationships between church and state. Thomas Jefferson termed this set of circumstances a "fair experiment" in his letter of reply to a group of Baptists in Virginia on November 21, 1808. Said Jefferson:

We have solved by fair experiment, the great and interesting question whether freedom of religion is compatible with order in government, and obedience to the laws. And we have experienced the quiet as well as the comfort which results from leaving everyone to profess freely and openly those principles of religion which are the inductions of his own reason, and the serious convictions of his own inquiries.[1]

Sidney E. Mead probably is more correct in describing the set of circumstances as "the lively experiment," since from the more recent perspective the shaping of Christianity in America has been characterized by innovation, frustration, competition, polemics, and, despite all, a measure of testing and retesting which has made the experiment seem to most Americans to be uniquely satisfactory and defensible.[2]

The testimony of the historians is rather clear on the point of the distinctiveness of American church disestablishment. Kenneth Scott Latourette, for example, declares: "The Christianity which developed in the United States [after 1800] was unique. It displayed features which marked it as distinct from previous Christianity in any other land." [3]

The embodiment of disestablishment in the American Constitution has been considered by another church historian "on the administrative side" as one of the "two most profound revolutions which have occurred in the entire history of the church." [4]

But, in a sense, everything is unique as far as history goes. From today's perspective the outlook of the apostle Paul seems to be unique, for he thought that the second coming of Christ and the end of the existing world order were so near that the creation of a genuine theory of church-state relations was not necessary. In his earlier writings he evidently believed that history would come to its close in his own lifetime.[5] Near the end of his life, Paul felt that he likely would die before the great event.[6] History did not come to an end, however, and Paul's views must, in historical perspective, be considered distinctive.

Similarly, the establishment of the imperial state church under Constantine must be viewed as distinctive. Constantine looked upon Christianity as an important means of consolidating the process of unification which had long been in progress in the Roman Empire. The empire had one law, one citizenship for all free men, and one emperor. Why should it not have one religion? Christianity, according to Constantine, was to be the unifying faith. So, in the first part of the fourth century Constantine began a series of actions which transformed the churches from objects of persecution by previous emperors into the official agencies of the Roman world. How surprised Paul would have been if he had lived to see that set of circumstances! How different they were from those which characterize the American tradition!

The truth of the matter, however, appears to be that church and state relations through the centuries have been marked by a multitude of unique experiments. While the tendency of American Christians (non-Christians, too) may be to view the American tradition as normative, the fact of the matter is that the long history of the relations of the Christian churches with the governments with which they have been confronted shows no single or simple pattern. The relationships are characterized by great diversity, and the beginning of wisdom in any consideration of the subject of church and state relations lies in the open recognition of this diversity. Within this diversity, the American tradition is simply one formation among others, and when viewing it from within, one finds almost every type and expression of relationship that has characterized the previous ages.

THEORETICAL EFFORTS

A number of theoretical efforts have been made in recent years to delineate the basic pattern or patterns of relationship between church and state. Paul Tillich, for example, attempting an analysis of the relationships of religion and culture, claims, among other things, that "religion is being ultimately concerned about that which is and should be our ultimate concern." The church is the communal and historical embodiment of the new reality which is brought within and under the conditions of man's predicament by Jesus. As such, "the unconditional claim made by Christianity is not related to the Christian Church, but to the event on which the Church is based." As a consequence, in Tillich's view, the gap between the sacred and the secular realms disappears. Religion and culture possess an identity. Says Tillich:

Religion as ultimate concern is the meaning-giving substance of culture, and culture is the totality of forms in which the basic concern of religion expresses itself. In abbreviation: religion is the substance of culture, culture is the form of religion. Such a consideration definitely prevents the establishment of a dualism of religion and culture. Every religious act, not only in organized religion, but also in the most intimate movement of the soul, is culturally formed.[7]

Tillich's view on the identity of religion and culture, however, scarcely throws light upon the dark scene of the contemporary questing for more wisdom regarding the existential relations between church and state. Probably Tillich, despite his Lutheran background, does not allow, in this aspect of his theory, sufficient distinction for the separation of the "orders" in society. From an Olympian perspective all social institutions may appear to possess an intrinsic harmony and mutuality. But viewed from the standpoint of newspaper case studies, for example, such as those reporting on decisions of the United States Supreme Court, the harmony and mutuality seem to be distant.

The late H. Richard Niebuhr struggled to formulate a set of theoretical patterns which would explain and interpret the relationships between "Christ and culture." Obviously, "Christ and culture" involves a quite different meaning from "religion and culture." Again, as will be seen later in some detail, both of these referents are different from the commonly employed language of "church and state." Niebuhr, however, carefully defines his basic terms before he goes on to classify the kinds of relations which have existed between Christ and culture. He finds five classical interpretations of the relationships, devoting a chapter in a book to each of them: (1) Christ against culture; (2) Christ of culture; (3) Christ above culture; (4) Christ and culture in paradox; and (5) Christ as the transformer of culture.

The first two types in Niebuhr's view are basically different. The first type emphasizes the opposition of Christ and culture. According to Niebuhr, "Whatever may be the customs of the society in which the Christian lives, and whatever the human achievements it conserves, Christ is seen as opposed to them, so that he confronts men with the challenge of an 'either-or' decision." The second recognizes a fundamental agreement between Christ and culture. Niebuhr states:

In our time answers of this kind are given by Christians who note the close relations between Christianity and Western civilization, between Jesus' teachings or the teachings about him and democratic institutions; yet there are occasional interpretations that emphasize the agreement between Christ and Eastern culture as well as some that tend to identify him with the spirit of Marxian society.

The other typical answers or patterns "agree with each

other in seeking to maintain the great differences between the two principles and in undertaking to hold them together in some unity." These differ from each other by the manner in which each seeks to combine the two authorities.[8]

Niebuhr's analysis is probably more helpful than Tillich's for those who in historical and sociological terms seek to trace the multitudinous variations which obviously exist between the two social institutions of church and state. His typology provides more categories into which the seemingly disparate facts of history and the contemporary scene can be catalogued. Also, Niebuhr's theory is genuinely theoretical, that is, it not only seeks to satisfy the quest for empirical understanding but also attempts to formulate intellectual constructs by which the whole phenomenon may be understood. Such concinnity is genuinely "abstractive," as this term was used by Alfred North Whitehead.[9]

PRESSING PERPLEXITIES

The kinds of analyses conducted by Tillich and Niebuhr are both needed and legitimate. Expositions of other classifications will be made later in this book, but, aside from them, there exist myriad perplexities which impinge upon individuals and organizations today with pressing immediacy. Their form, moreover, is usually concrete rather than theoretical, and they call for decision rather than contemplation. A recounting of all of these "practical" problems need not be attempted, but the mere listing of some of them may help to illumine the concreteness and the immediacy of the current situation.

Their listing is for illustrative purposes, and intends no prejudice toward possible "answers":

1. Should Peace Corps workers engage in church-sponsored projects abroad?

2. Should church-related hospitals accept federal subsidies (the Hill-Burton Hospital Survey and Construction Act)?

3. Should church-related agencies accept governmental subsidies to cover the cost of erecting housing for old people?

4. Should churches accept the state and local governmental subsidies now provided for "purchase of service" plans?

5. Should church institutions and camping programs serving children receive surplus food on much the same basis as do public school lunchrooms?

6. Should church organizations, such as Church World Service, be given governmental surplus food for distribution abroad?

7. Should churches and their institutions secure special benefits in government-subsidized urban renewal programs?

8. Should the laws in several states which require that adoptive placement of children be only in homes of the same religious faith as that of the parents of the children be continued?

9. Should transportation to church schools, as is provided at public expense in sixteen states (and in part in five additional states), be maintained?

10. Should free textbooks be furnished to children in church schools, as they are now in five states?

11. Should the churches be exempt from customary

taxes on businesses and enjoy such privileges as monopoly on gambling or lotteries, relief from standards applied to restaurants, legalized discounts on travel, exemption from excise taxes, waiving of building fees, exemptions on labor standards and public liability, preferential postage rates?

12. Should direct state aid, involving outright grants, for tuition, scholarships, or loans for church school construction, be accepted by the churches?

13. Should clergymen and nuns, when qualified, be permitted to teach in the public schools while wearing distinctive religious garb?

14. Should Bible reading and prayer be permitted in governmentally provided schools?

15. Should the public schools observe the religious holidays of any religious group?

16. Should baccalaureate services be held in the public schools?

17. Should the public schools utilize any distinctively religious symbols, such as a crucifix, a nativity creche, or a menorah, on their property?

18. Should religion in any form be taught in the public schools?

19. Should school credit for courses in religion, wherever held, be given?

20. Should the public schools provide vocational tests and counseling for religious vocations?

21. Should compulsory or voluntary R.O.T.C. programs be a part of church-related colleges?

22. Should the individual be required to salute the flag of the United States?

23. Should religious individuals and groups be permitted to disobey laws that are deemed necessary to pro-

tect the health and safety of society as a whole, such as those pertaining to vaccinations?

24. Should some plan for weekday religious education, such as "dismissed time," "released time," or "shared time," be permitted?

25. Should the religious person be allowed to witness to his convictions as an employee of a public organization?

26. Does the absence of governmental support for religious organizations tend to create "the peril of culture-religion"?

27. Should religious activities always be based upon voluntarism?

28. What is the nature of the church as a social institution?

29. What is the nature of the state as a social institution?

30. What is religious freedom?

31. What is civil liberty?

32. How can a "public philosophy" be formed in a religiously pluralistic society?

33. What is the Biblical understanding of the relations of church and state?

34. Can the concept of "natural law" throw light on the relations between church and state?

The above listing of questions suggests that twentieth-century America is faced with a complicated set of circumstances to which its heritage has brought it and that the problems are manifold and difficult to solve, requiring patient, objective, and skilled treatment. These problems press on individuals and their organizations to a degree that has stimulated a fresh and massive effort on the part of many, both secular and religious, to attempt scientific understanding. While "solutions" to such questions as those posed above are being sought regularly through the courts of the land, it is clear that suitable "answers" rest ultimately not upon legal decisions alone, but upon a broader and deeper understanding of the American tradition and its possibilities now and in the future.

Greater understanding of the complicated relations between the social institutions of church and state is urgently needed; and such understanding, moreover, pertains not to a narrow band of interests and relations on the part of a select number of people, but is relevant to the whole texture of American society. Many studies are needed just to clarify the relationships between church and state. Many of these efforts, reflecting a wide diversity of starting points and conclusions, have been made or are under way. Taken together, they will, it is hoped, produce a truth or truths that will be both constructive and enduring.

TENSIONS AND CONFLICTS

In the past, and perhaps to a lessening degree in recent years, the differences in the "answers" to the basic questions regarding church and state, such as those listed above, have led to observable tensions and even conflicts among the several religious groups and others within pluralistic America. Especially keen at certain times and places have been the differences of policies and practices between Protestant and Roman Catholic Christians. Yet it probably would be unfair to claim that this interreligious conflict was based solely upon differing conceptions of the relationships of church and state.

Robert McAfee Brown, a Protestant, writing in a Roman Catholic publication, helpfully delineates six main types of opposition to Catholicism on the part of anti-Catholics, showing that the issues far transcend that of church and state relations. Brown's six main types of opposition to Catholicism are as follows:

(1) The "if-they're-for-it-I'm-against-it" person, who has an entirely negative creed, lacks positive convictions of his own faith, and opposes pope, saints, priests, purgatory, parochial schools, and Catholics who run for public office.

(2) The Protestant "bigot" who cultivates all the "facts," with special reference to the "dirt" about Catholics. He knows the worst, and will not listen to the best about them, calling fellow Protestants who have a good word for Catholics naïve or misinformed.

(3) The "when-they-get-to-the-majority-they'll-destroy-our-freedom" group, who collect data on persecutions of Protestants in Italy, Spain, Colombia, and Argentina. They know little about those American Catholics (whom they consider a negligible minority) who are concerned for civil liberties and who publicly disavow Catholics who advocate seizure of secular power.

(4) Those who fear the "vast-monolithic-structure" of the Catholic Church and believe it to have members of one mind, one vote, and one fear of democracy.

(5) The "Catholicism-is-clericalism" type, who reasons that all Catholics are anti-American gamblers and drunkards who believe Protestants are going to hell, because he sees the local priest promote bingo, use wine in the Mass, teach Roman Catholicism as the only true religion, and raise funds for the parochial school.

(6) The type who sees his own religion as a positive heritage and takes issue with Catholics on the basis of

Christian convictions, in an effort to be faithful to the Gospel.[10]

Thus, while tensions and conflicts between Protestants and Roman Catholics do exist on the basis of differences of viewpoint on the relations between church and state, they historically and at present rest upon a larger and more complex configuration of intergroup relationships. Common agreements, therefore, on "solutions" to the problems of church and state will not of themselves completely eliminate such intergroup conflicts, although every gain in cooperation helps reduce tensions.

Similarly, there are tensions and conflicts among the several Protestant communions, some of which relate to issues of church and state. John C. Bennett is correct when he says, "There is no Protestant doctrine concerning Church-State relations." [11] What is to be inferred from his statement is that there is no over-all, single, uniform Protestant doctrine regarding the relations of church and state. Some communions, it is true, have only recently come to realize that they have failed to develop systematic statements on the subject, and some of them are currently overcoming this lack. But, in actuality, the several communions have at least implicit positions on the subject. These positions often are developed and applied in a pragmatic or piecemeal fashion, taking each particular problem in turn as it becomes vexing. To the extent to which intergroup tension and conflict exist within Protestantism in the United States, however, the presence of unresolved differences of policy and practice on the subject of church and state must be supposed to be an important causative factor. Any success on the part of the Protestant communions in resolving their differences regarding the relations of church and state well might increase opportunities generally for mutual understanding and cooperation.

On this score, Sam Duker has some sage comments:

What is needed in our society as a whole . . . is a spirit of understanding and consideration toward those who hold religious views different from or even contrary to our own. Such a spirit must go far beyond that of tolerance for diverse views. A spirit of accommodation is, of course, as necessary on the part of those holding minority views as it is on the part of those professing generally accepted beliefs and views. Recriminations and reproaches will not solve any portion of our problem but frank discussions may.[12]

The National Study Conference on Church and State, sponsored by the Department of Religious Liberty of the National Council of the Churches of Christ in the United States of America, held in Columbus, Ohio, in February, 1964, involving Protestant and Orthodox churches, contributed significantly to the sharing of diverse opinions and practices and to the limited formulation of common perspectives on the relations of church and state.

A number of communions, among them the Methodist Church, the United Presbyterian Church in the United States of America, and the Lutheran Church in America, through special commissions and church bodies have studied and published their own policy statements on the subject. Despite all these efforts, however, much remains to be done.

SOCIAL INSTITUTIONS

In 1963 the Commission on Church and State Relations in a Pluralistic Society of the Board of Social Ministry of the Lutheran Church in America published a statement entitled *Church and State: a Lutheran Perspective.* The final section of that report is summarized as follows (in italics in the original document): "We shall defend both the institutional separation and the functional inter-action of church and state in the United States and Canada." Also, says the report, "Americans and Canadians live in free lands which, while recognizing the institutional separation of church and state, nevertheless also favor a functional inter-action which is mutually beneficial." [13] Unfortunately, however, the Lutheran Church in America document nowhere develops a definition of the church and the state as social institutions. It is to this task that the remainder of this chapter is devoted.

The nature and variety of social institutions have been studied in anthropological theory by those who advocate "functionalism." Among the functionalists, the teachings of Bronislaw Malinowski probably are most detailed and helpful.[14]

Malinowski taught that culture is composed of the dynamic interrelationships between three factors: human needs, social institutions, and "synthetic imperatives."

The human being possesses certain fundamental, physiological needs. These require organized, collective responses from society. Among these needs are food, shelter, safety, relaxation, movement, growth, and reproduction. The organized response to these "basic imperatives" accounts for the social organization of society. The family, for example, exists for the satisfaction of affectional and reproductive needs. The needs of man for food, shelter, dress, and other material comfort constitute the basis for the economic system, which is concerned with production, processing, and exchange. According to this view, no aspect of the social organization of society exists for a self-justifying purpose. All institutions of society are based upon the validity and urgency of human needs.

The needs of human individuals constitute the foundation of the social institutions. All institutions are responsive primarily to the persistent wants of men. All of them —economic, political, legal, educational, familial, social, and others—exist for the satisfaction of human needs. The social institutions or some parts of them may be moribund for periods of time. Ultimately, however, a social institution cannot continue to exist without in some measure satisfying human needs.

The social institutions are formed and exist in order to serve the fundamental and limited interests of human beings. Some social scientists, for example, have concluded that there are essentially four major interests and their resulting institutions in all societies. These are the economic and governmental systems (concerned with the food supply, property, class, and law systems); the family (concerned with courtship, marriage, divorce, training of the young, and treatment of the aged); aesthetic and intellectual expressions and recreational needs (which find outlet in dancing, acting, poetry, art, science, philosophy, social activities, games, and entertainment), and religion, with its accompanying beliefs and practices.

Other social scientists, however, have concluded that the social institutions, as well as the basic needs from which they are derived, are far more numerous. Joyce Hertzler, for instance, classified the social institutions in nine major categories.[15] Other social scientists claim that there is an almost endless number of social institutions. But, no matter how the social institutions may be classified, their distinctiveness rests upon the assumption that each possesses a unique set of functions or activities by which it is characterized and differentiated from other social institutions. Implicit in the very nature of each social institution is a system of concerted activities by which its coherence and quasi autonomy are asserted and maintained. In fact, a more complete definition would state that a social institution is a system of concerted activities carried on by an organized and specifically designated group of persons who operate under a charter, in accordance with definite rules, and by means of a material apparatus. Each of these four components of the fuller definition gives a basis to the distinctiveness of each of the social institutions in society.

From this standpoint, then, both the church and the state exist as social institutions, brought into being to satisfy basic human needs and maintained in differing degrees of separateness in order that they may fulfill those human and social functions which society has ascribed to them. To say that they are "separate" does not mean that they are necessarily opposed, but simply that they have been established to fulfill different human functions in society.

At times there are discussions of aspects or qualities of social institutions which assume that the process of institutionalization has not occurred or that it is not a determinative factor in the understanding of the aspects or the qualities. "Political power," for example, may be torn from its institutional moorings and discussed at great length in abstract terms. But political power, as the anthropologist knows it, always occurs within an institutional context. One must relate "political power" to the particular institutional forms which make it possible and whose limitations as social realities determine the nature of this aspect of a political institution. So, too, in religion. Some groups claim to be "merely a fellowship, not a denomination," or they extol a particular practice as though it could somehow escape from its institutional limitations. For example, Donald G. Miller says: "The church is a fellowship of faith, not an institution." [16]

H. Paul Douglass and Edmund deS. Brunner discuss the impossibility of noninstitutionalized religion:

Those most critical of what they consider the institutionalism of the church themselves exhibit it. Sects, for example, like the primitive Baptist, representing extreme anti-ecclesiastical attitudes, maintaining the utmost simplicity and freedom in worship and an unpaid ministry are genuinely shocked by the excesses of the Holy Rollers as the latter appear in mountain communities. Yet the truth is that the mountain preacher who most loudly proclaims that he receives his sermon by direct inspiration of God is asserting a highly-developed religious convention. Even in the most informal intercourse of his group he is subject to the dead hand of social ritualism. . . . The attempt, then, to conceive of a non-institutionalized religion for modern man is sociologically infantile. It is an attack on rationality and ethical stability themselves. Religion cannot have currency without developing some generalized form, and generalized form implies habits resistant to change which are the essence of institutionalization.[17]

A religious group may initially possess a relatively low degree of institutionalization, but steadily, if not perceptibly, the institutionalization will grow. With its growth, moreover, a somewhat different social institution is realized. Walter G. Muelder illustrates this point by quoting the minister of a Pentecostal sect called the Bethel Assembly of God:

We are going through the same process as the Methodists did. We are in the cycle. We are gradually giving more attention to the form of government, controlled by the bishops, and following formal services. If divisions come it will be over these matters. The younger churches will say, 'let us go out into the highways and bring them in,' whereas the formal churches will say, 'They know where we are; let them come to us.' That is the picture of what is taking place in my own denomination.[18]

The various communions in the United States—Protestant, Orthodox, Roman Catholic, Jewish, and others—are in the main far from the situation of the Bethel Assembly of God. They are highly developed social institutions with notably complex sets of specialized functions which are maintained by an extensive corps of workers, with voluminous statements of policies and procedures (their charters) and with the support of property investments which run into the hundreds of millions of dollars.

Lest the institutional limitations placed upon "pure and undefiled religion" seem an impossible burden for the spirit of man to bear, it is well to note the theological insight developed by H. Richard Niebuhr to the effect that God has chosen to be present in human affairs, but always in limited form. God may be unlimited, but his expressions in human affairs are always less than unlimited. The Judeo-Christian doctrine of creation provides ample explication of God's purpose to be limited by the manifold forms that he creates. The Christian doctrine of the incarnation, moreover, strengthens this insight even at the point where God is assumed to have taken human form.

Social institutions, then, may be viewed not only as a social necessity, especially in anthropological terms, but also as a divinely elected requirement. From this perspective the social institutions are not simply intransigent social forms that organize and limit men's social activities, but necessary social forms that provide advantages and opportunities to those values which men hold most dear.

The conception of church and state as social institutions, in the anthropological manner, is further developed in the following chapters and in the last chapter is cautiously applied to the current situation.

2

Changing Perspectives:
The Church

KEY TERMS

William Lee Miller supports the view that it is difficult
to classify the relation of religion to society in America in
traditionally historical and sociological ways. Says Miller:

The relation of religion to society in America is neither that
of the 'sect' nor that of the 'church'; it is something new.
Though the 'sect' element is very important, the mainstream of
religion here has not emphasized repudiation of the princi-
palities and power of this world or withdrawal from society
in order to preserve ethical purity and holiness . . . This
tradition countenances no desire for a 'religious' state or even
an officially religious society; it does, however, want a religious
people and an unofficially religious society. The individuals
are religious, the state is not.[1]

To comprehend Miller, however, calls for a considerable
understanding not only of American history but of the
ways in which sociologists and others have classified religious groups. Key terms in Miller's analysis, from which
the American heritage differs, he claims, are "church" and
"sect."

Sidney E. Mead employs a somewhat different terminology in his historically oriented analysis of American Christianity. He claims that "the denomination is the organizational form which the free churches have accepted and assumed." The denominational form, however, is institutionally unique, according to Mead:

The basis of the institutional uniqueness has been the free church idea. The phrase, free churches, is used in various ways—sometimes to designate those churches of congregational polity, sometimes those peculiarly distinguished by their liberal views. But properly the phrase designates those churches under the system of separation of church and state. Here the qualifying word "free" is used in the sense of independent and autonomous and in the context of long tradition refers to those churches that are independent of the state and autonomous in relation to it.[2]

Mead's description of the nature of the group life of religion in America also utilizes key terms, such as "the denomination" and "free churches." These terms, like Miller's, stand in a long and serious tradition of social analysis. This tradition merits some review, both as a means of extending and enriching the notion of the church as a social institution and as a means of giving systematic recognition to the seemingly manifold types of religious groupings that have occurred in the American, and indeed in the Western, heritage.

CLASSIFICATIONS

Many efforts have been made to classify the churches. They vary considerably in seriousness and utility.

Quietistic and Activistic Classifications

One classification, for example, contrasts churches in terms of polar qualities: quietistic and activistic. On the basis of such a distinction, church historians have claimed, for instance, that American churches tend to be more activistic than European churches. The latter are more quietistic.[3] A similar analysis was made of American urban churches by the Institute of Social and Religious Research.[4] The value of this classification for an understanding of church and state is minimal, however, because it rests on only one factor of analysis.

Polity

Churches also have been classified according to the three basic organizational forms in which they are found: the episcopal, the presbyterian, and the congregational. These types correspond roughly and respectively to the political forms of monarchies, aristocracies, and democracies. In the episcopal form, churches are organized in a hierarchical manner. Authority rests in the higher offices and persons, and the local congregation has little control over the clergy and other matters. The Roman Catholic Church is an illustration of episcopal polity.

The presbyterian form of church organization is intermediate between the episcopal and the congregational. In it church organization is controlled by the constituent church bodies (synods and presbyteries), and local congregations are dominated by elders. Clergymen in the presbyterian system have dual obligations—to the elders of the local church and to the presbyteries and synods. The

United Presbyterian Church in the United States of America is an example of presbyterian polity.

In the congregational organization, the members of local congregations are collectively the source of authority. Church organization beyond the local congregation is loosely organized and at many points lacks authentic authority. The clergyman of the local congregation, being selected solely by the local congregation, serves as a democratic leader. The American Baptist Convention is an example of congregational polity.

These three types of church organization do not often appear in pure form, since, aside from being "ideal types," they also have been greatly modified in America by significant social tendencies toward increased democratization of all social institutions. In a few instances, moreover, no one of the three organizational forms seems to be appropriate (witness, for example, the military organization of the Salvation Army). These three forms, furthermore, do not in themselves bear a fundamental relationship to principles governing the relations of the churches to the state.

Church and Sect

By now one of the most familiar and important of the classifications of the churches is that developed by the German theologian and historian, Ernst Troeltsch. It is to his classification of "church" and "sect" that William Lee Miller, mentioned earlier, referred. Troeltsch's classification of two main types of ecclesiastical organizations has been widely employed in discussions of the relations of church and state, and is worthy of conscientious attention. Although Troeltsch's church-sect typology probably was influenced by the thought of Max Weber, with whom he lived for a time, Troeltsch himself is responsible for the articulate and systematic analysis of the two main types of church organization.[5]

The church, in Troeltsch's terms, readily accepts the secular order of society. Its strategy in relation to society is one of compromise. In theory it claims to be superior, separate, and dominant; but in practice it is quite willing to compromise its autonomic claims for the benefits which accrue to it from its also being a basic defender of the existing power arrangements. This type of church organization shuns absolutist positions on all matters; it is willing to compromise with the secular powers in order to maintain and extend its general influence in society.

The church is the religious organization for all of the people. The citizen is born into the church; he does not elect to become a member of it. The church is not a voluntary membership organization, but is a universal institution whose existence is a *sine qua non* of social existence. Troeltsch thought that the church is highly dependent upon the state and the ruling classes for its existence and influence in society, that the church both stabilizes and determines the social order, and that its life is characterized by careful organization and institutional stability.

The fundamental emphasis of the church, so far as its inner life is concerned, is upon sacrament and creed. This emphasis, mediated through the clergy, tends to lay a minimal emphasis upon the moral demands of religion, since salvation depends not upon ethical achievement but upon the reception of the sacraments and acquiescence to the creeds. The church tends to be relatively moderate in its discipline; it is more ready to exclude persons who question the creedal and sacramental basis for the faith than it is to condemn those who fail to realize its ethical standards.

The sect, by contrast, is defined in terms that are largely opposite to those of the church. The sect is less than universal; in fact, its membership is comparatively small. Those who belong are not born into the church, but have joined voluntarily—commonly as a result of a decisive experience or "new birth." Because of the necessity for voluntary membership in the sect, the emphasis in this type of religious organization is upon direct personal relationships with God. Creeds and sacraments are minimized, and the emphasis is upon individual emotional experience and ethical behavior.

Max Weber early observed that sect membership in the business world has been taken as the equivalent of a certificate of moral qualification. Sectarians seek to differentiate themselves from "hypocrites" and "heretics." [6]

Sects are critical both of the existing church and of the social order. They criticize the rigidity of ecclesiastical structure, the ability of generalized religion to satisfy the needs of individuals, the failure of the church regularly to translate its sacramental and creedal practices into new symbols and meanings, and the allegedly low moral standards of the churches' members. Sects tend to believe that no religious organization can dominate the world. Often they do not even think it desirable that the church dominate the state, since they tend to hold negative estimates of both church and state.

Sectarian members stress a literal obedience to the Scriptures and seek to emulate primitive church ideals. They find their chief satisfactions in their own emotional experiences and the sense of communion developed within their memberships. The sect, in Troeltsch's view, finds its membership in the lower classes. These by definition do not have the same stake in the universality of religious forms and in the sanctification of the existing social order that the upper classes have.

Troeltsch aptly lists the basic characteristics of the sect:

. . . lay Christianity, personal achievement in ethics and in religion, the radical fellowship of love, religious equality and brotherly love, indifference toward the authority of the State and the ruling classes, dislike of technical law and of the oath, the separation of the religious life from the economic struggle by means of the ideal of poverty and frugality . . . , the directness of the personal religious relationship, criticism of official spiritual guides and theologians, the appeal to the New Testament and the Primitive Church.[7]

Troeltsch also presented a third type of Christian thought, mysticism, in contradistinction to church and sect. This type does not depend upon the all-embracing importance of the social organization of the church; it does not depend upon the "communion of the saints" characteristic of the sect. Mysticism, in Troeltsch's view, depends upon a high degree of individualism in which personal experiences are supreme. Mysticism as a form of Christian thought creates no permanent organization, neither church or sect. Troeltsch sought not only to differentiate among the forms of religious organizations in Christianity, but also to utilize these distinctions as a means to classify the social teaching of the Christian churches. Thus, his third type is more pertinent to the classification of the social teachings than it is to an understanding of the nature of the social institutions which have comprised Western Christianity.

Also, Troeltsch was quite willing to recognize that his three types of the Christian religion are "ideal" types and that they in no way constitute an imposition of a rigid classification upon concrete and discrete religious reality. Said Troeltsch: "In actual life, of course, these different types mingle and combine with each other, just as the different types of Christian fellowship also mingle and combine. But this abstract analysis makes the history of dogma much clearer and simpler." [8]

Wach's Classification

Troeltsch's able and significant typology has been criticized and amended often in the last half century. Joachim Wach, for example, on the basis of extensive study has concluded that there are three major forms of Christian religious organizations: (1) ecclesiastical bodies, (2) independent bodies, and (3) sectarian bodies. The ecclesiastical bodies (such as Lutherans, Calvinists, and Anglicans) have authoritatively defined doctrines, sacraments, and orders. Their appeal is to the one, invisible church of all the ages. The independent bodies (such as Baptists, Quakers, Disciples) are less institutional and lay more stress upon the value of Christian fellowship. Sectarian bodies (such as Mennonites, Brethren, and Pentecostal groups) emphasize disciplined individual conduct and the significance of a qualitatively intense congregational association, with feelings of indifference or hostility toward other types of church organization and toward society in general.

Wach's classification is similar to that of Troeltsch, although the precise categories are also reminiscent of the episcopal-presbyterian-congregational typology. As with Troeltsch's classification of religious bodies, Wach's throws considerable light upon the variety of relationships that

are possible both in theory and in historical actuality between church and state.[9]

Yinger's Classification

J. Milton Yinger recently has provided a review of
Troeltsch's typology that is helpful, especially from the
standpoint of functional analysis. Yinger's criticism of
Troeltsch's typology takes two forms. First, he claims that
Troeltsch failed to provide an adequate picture of the full
range of religious organizations evident in Western Christianity, even when the concept of mysticism is employed.
Second, he criticizes Troeltsch for failing to testify suffi-
ciently to the personality and social factors which are
connected with the various types of religious organization.
Yinger, although deeply indebted to Troeltsch, bases his
own typology upon "the degree of inclusiveness of the
members of a society and the degree of attention to the
function of social integration as contrasted with the function of personal need." [10]

As a consequence, Yinger suggests a sixfold classification
of religious organizations, the first three of which are ap-
proximately equivalent to Troeltsch's church type; the
latter three, roughly equivalent to his sect type. Yinger's
major forms are (1) the universal church, (2) the ecclesia,
(3) the class church or denomination, (4) the established
sect, (5) the sect, and (6) the cult.

The universal church is relatively successful in supporting the integration of a society. It also is able, through
beliefs and observances, to satisfy the personality needs
of individuals on all levels of the society. The Roman
Catholic Church of the thirteenth century is considered to
be the best illustration of a universal church in Western

civilization, since it was relatively effective in meeting the individualizing tendencies in Christianity through the monasteries, while its formalized system of beliefs and rituals was able to meet the religious requirements of large numbers of the people of its day.

The ecclesia is a form of religious organization which Yinger borrowed as a category from Howard Becker.[11] The ecclesia, like the universal church, reaches out to all levels of society, but in doing so it tends to become overly adjusted to the dominant elements of the society and fails to satisfy the individual needs of many of its adherents, especially those from the lower classes. The ecclesia might be called a universal church in a state of rigidification. The Russian Orthodox Church of 1915 provides an illustration of the ecclesia form.

The class church or denomination is less successful in achieving universality than the ecclesia and the universal church, even though it may be substantially in harmony with the secular power structure. The class church or denomination is limited by class, racial, and sometimes regional boundaries, and possesses sectarian elements despite the fact that all class levels tend to be represented in its membership. The class church or denomination commonly begins as a sect and has failed to a notable degree to escape its sect origins. Some class churches, like the Congregational, possess fairly persistent sectarian tendencies, while others, like the Lutheran, are more thoroughly accommodated to the secular social order.

The established sect developed out of sects and cults. Although the original concern of the established sects was chiefly with the evils of society, they have developed that degree of formal organization and acceptance of society which seeks both to recognize some values of the society while opposing others and, in addition, to continue to stress individual regeneration on the part of those who are burdened with anxiety, doubt, and suffering. Methodism and Christian Science clearly are established sects.

The sect, in Yinger's view, is likely to meet socially undesirable conditions in one of three ways: (1) acceptance, (2) aggression, or (3) avoidance. Some sects, such as Moral Re-Armament, accept the secular social order but believe that an evil society can be improved through the individual's overcoming of personal sins and failings. Other sects, such as the early Anabaptists, representing lower-class interests, believe that aggression against an evil society through programs of social reform constitutes the basis for religious organization. More often, however, sects protest social evils by withdrawing from society and projecting the hopes of their members into a future, perfect world. The present life of the membership is strengthened and satisfied individually through the forming and maintenance of a strongly knit "communion of the saints," as is evident in the Holiness, Pentecostal, and Adventist groups.

The cult, finally, tends to be small in membership and unrelated to other cult bodies. Often its existence depends upon the leadership of a charismatic personality and, as a consequence, tends to be short-lived. The energies of the cult are concentrated almost exclusively upon the problems of the individual rather than upon those of the social order. Yinger concludes that "perhaps the best examples are the various Spiritualist groups and some of the 'Moslem' groups among American Negroes." [12]

STRUCTURAL COMPLEXITIES

The several typologies of religious organization, almost solely pertinent to Christianity in the West, have not been presented with the purpose of settling once and for all the general and precise problems of cultural analysis which they involve. Such an exposition is entirely worthy, but must be conducted in a different context. The purpose behind the presentation here of the several typologies is that of extending and enriching the understanding of the relations between church and state. The church is a social institution with the attributes ascribed to it in the previous chapter. But, as a social institution, it assumes more than one structural form and functional aim. Whether the religious organization is a church or a sect does not cancel out its being a social institution. The description of the social institution of the church, however, as church or sect, or some variation of these basic categories, does add measurably to an understanding of the relations of church and state, for, as the preceding discussion has shown, the church or sect character of the religious organization determines (even as it is determined by) the more precise kinds of relationships that churches can have with states. The explication of these relationships will be taken up in chapters 5 and 6. At this point, however, it is well to realize that the nature of the relations of church and state is conditioned by the fact that the church and state are social institutions and that, furthermore, the kinds of social institutions the church and the state are, greatly determine the types of relationships that can exist between them.

Everywhere these relations are seen in institutional and relativistic forms; nowhere are they seen in single, universal, ideal or permanent form.

The several typologies of the nature of religious organization, moreover, instruct in the fact that the social institutions of the church and the state do not exist simply and solely in order to have relationships with one another. The basic functions of the church extend far beyond that of being related to the state; similarly, the state does not exist simply and solely to be related to the church. The fact is that both are social institutions with different functions. In performing their functions, they are related to one another even as the functions of all social institutions necessarily secure their cogency by contributing to the coherence and viability of the social order in general. In this sense, the confrontation of church and state historically and sociologically needs to be viewed from the wider perspective of Christianity and politics or religion and government. Only on the basis of a more comprehensive view of the relations of church and state can even these relations be fully and adequately understood.

THE CHANGING CHURCH

The church, both in its general and in its particular forms, is not a static social institution. Social institutions never are static. The church, like the other social institutions, is marked by change. This change at times seems imperceptible, but at some junctures it appears to be rapid and fundamental. The changeability of the church is an important clue to understanding its durability. But its dynamic character also conditions any tendency to discuss the relations of church and state in abstract formulations.

Three kinds of general social change involving the church will now be described to indicate some of the ways in which the church is not a static institution: (1) mobility on the church-sect continuum, (2) secularization, and (3) historical movement.

Mobility on the Church-Sect Continuum

H. Richard Niebuhr described the first of these changes in a book aptly entitled *The Social Sources of Denominationalism*.[13] Niebuhr provided a theory of the life history of religious bodies by describing a process by which cults originate, grow into sects, change into denominations, and finally develop into churches. Niebuhr shows that each succeeding generation within a sect-type religious organization tends to bring to the organization those personal and social attributes which encourage the sect to move on to become a church-type organization. Thus Niebuhr's thesis is that variations in ethics, polity, and theology among the various religious organizations have their roots

. . . in the relationship of the religious life to the cultural and political conditions prevailing in any group of Christians. . . . The exigencies of church discipline, the demands of the national psychology, the effect of social tradition, the influence of cultural heritage, and the weight of economic interest play their role in the definition of religious truth.[14]

Anton T. Boisen has applied Niebuhr's theory to the churches of Monroe County, Indiana. There he found that the Methodists, Disciples, and Baptists at first were vital groups which insisted upon first-hand religious experience. In their original forms they were marked by vigorous missionary zeal by which they grew in numerical and organizational strength. But over a period of 120 years they became "respectable." The original believers were succeeded by their more prosperous and socially conforming children. The "prophetic forward movements" were "leveled down and conventionalized." As this process continued, new sects grew up in the same spontaneous and emotional way that the other groups had a century earlier.[15] The findings of Elmer T. Clark and others also tend to confirm Niebuhr's thesis that there is mobility on the church-sect continuum.[16]

Secularization

The increasing secularization of the church must be viewed as a part of a comprehensive trend in American society generally. Secularization occurs when theological and mythical explanations of man, society, and the universe are displaced by naturalistic explanations. Those who accept secularization as a broad-scale (general and religious) movement tend to agree with Emile Durkheim that history clearly teaches "that religion tends to embrace a smaller and smaller portion of social life. Originally, it pervades everything; everything social is religious . . . Then, little by little, political, economic, scientific functions free themselves from the religious function . . ."[17]

Similarly, Gordon W. Allport and his associates concluded from a study of college students that when religious group members change their church affiliation, they almost invariably move toward a more liberal position, toward "ethical but not theological Christianity."[18]

The most popular of the current celebrants of the process of secularization is Harvey Cox. In a widely read

book, Cox claims that the two hallmarks of our era are
the rise of urban civilization and the collapse of traditional religion. Secularization is the pervasive social process which is making formal religion irrelevant. According
to Cox:

Secularization simply bypasses and undercuts religion and
goes on to other things. It has relativized religious world-
views and thus rendered them innocuous. Religion has been
privatized. It has been accepted as the peculiar prerogative
and point of view of a particular person or group. Secularization has accomplished what fire and chain could not: It has
convinced the believer that he could be wrong, and persuaded the devotee that there are more important things than
dying for the faith . . . the age of the secular city . . . no
longer looks to religious rules and rituals for its morality or
its meanings. For some religion provides a hobby, for others a
mark of national or ethnic identification, for still others an
esthetic delight. For fewer and fewer does it provide an inclusive and commanding system of personal and cosmic values
and explanations.[19]

On the other hand the forceful views of Harvey Cox
have brought into being a whole host of sharp critics who
believe that he overestimates the power of the process of
secularization. The validity of Cox's views is warmly debated on both theological and sociological grounds.[20]

The increasing secularization of the church is merely
one expression of the manifold ways in which the church
is influenced by the standards and practices of society.
John C. Bennett notes this fact in his discussion of T. S.
Eliot's *The Idea of a Christian Society*. Bennett remarks
that Eliot's book "could not have been written for this
country as Mr. Eliot clearly recognizes and therefore it

provides some illumination for us by contrast." [21] Similarly, in discussing the major characteristics of Roman Catholicism "which are usually neglected in American discussions of the problem of Catholic power and yet which may make a difference in our conclusions about it," Bennett notes

. . . its great variations from culture to culture and from country to country. The vision of many American Protestants of a monolithic Roman Church, built somewhat on the lines of the Stalinist empire, that is controlled from the Vatican is very wide of the mark. Historically, it has proved itself capable of adjustment to the greatest variety of cultural conditions instead of being one kind of religious ethos exported from Rome. [22]

In these ways Bennett indicates how adaptable religion (in this case a Christian church) is to the various and diverse cultures in which it finds itself.

In this connection, it is worth noting that a careful study of the church and its ministry by H. Richard Niebuhr and his associates concluded that the modern organizational environment has significantly influenced the manner in which the churches, despite their policy, are organized. Says Niebuhr:

As the polity of all the churches, whether they are episcopal, presbyterian or congregational by tradition, has been modified in the direction of the political structures of Canada and the United States, so the institutional status and authority of the ministry are being modified in the direction of the democratic type of political, educational and economic executive or managerial authority. [23]

Especially as the Protestant minister is respected and obeyed in his role as pastoral director, in conformity with patterns of executive leadership developed elsewhere in society, he is today, especially in the modified church-type and sect-type religious organizations, considered to be a significant community leader.[24]

In recent years the thought of Harvey Cox and others has made "secularization" a popular term among religious people. Basing his thought upon the contributions of Dietrich Bonhoeffer, Friedrich Gogarten, and others, Cox asserts that secularization is not an antireligious process, but "arises in large measure from the formative influence of biblical faith on the world, an influence mediated first by the Christian church and later by movements deriving partly from it." [25] Like many others, however, Cox clearly differentiates secularization from secularism. On this score, he says:

Secularization implies a historical process, almost certainly irreversible, in which society and culture are delivered from tutelage to religious control and closed metaphysical world-views. We have argued that it is basically a liberating development. Secularism, on the other hand, is the name for an ideology, a new closed world-view which functions very much like a new religion. While secularization finds its roots in the biblical faith itself and is to some extent an authentic outcome of the impact of biblical faith on Western history, this is not the case with secularism. Like any other ism, it menaces the openness and freedom secularization has produced; it must therefore be watched carefully to prevent its becoming the ideology of a new establishment.[26]

But the influence of society on the church is neither unitive or a one-way street. The church as a social institution bears its own testimony, in theory and practice, to the other social institutions of conceptions and practices which it both cherishes and finds to be effective. The church, while being influenced by society, also is a potent social force. James Hastings Nichols, for example, argues that while most of the forms of the Christian heritage have been unfavorable to democracy, modern democracy itself is dependent chiefly upon the Calvinistic and the left-wing sectarian traditions, both of which he terms "Puritan Protestantism." If he is correct, and there is a strong presumption that he is, Nichols has laid a solid basis for concluding that the church, at least in some of its forms, has had a decided influence upon the social institution of democratic government. His views, however, need to be tempered by the historical consideration of other sources which contributed to the formation of democracy.[27]

Historical Movement

The third illustration of the dynamic character of the church as a social institution is the historical movement which has basically modified its relations to society and even to its own nature. One form of such historical movement will be briefly mentioned. There has been the change in American history from, in the words of Franklin Littell, "state church to pluralism." [28] Littell boldly describes the manner in which the colonial state churches were in part unable to and in part did not want to maintain their privileged positions in society. He recounts the several religious and secular forces developed in the various periods of American history that resulted in religious pluralism in which all varieties of religious organizations were recognized, even officially, as voluntary organizations based upon persuasion rather than coercion. In summarizing the situation of the colonial state churches, Littell states:

. . . We have a colonial record in New England with an oppressive establishment of mixed Congregational and Presbyterian order, with an internal inconsistency carrying the seeds of its own destruction. In the southern colonies, Anglicanism enjoyed up to the time of the Revolution a position of privilege, which—when it collapsed—left whole sections of the population unchurched. In New York State the picture was more ambiguous, although both Friends and Presbyterians were compelled to fight for their rights under the Anglican establishment. Only in Pennsylvania, and the colonies which for some time shared its history (the Jerseys and Delaware), was the shift to religious liberty and voluntary support accomplished without severe readjustment. Pennsylvania, indeed, despised by New Englanders and southerners alike as a 'swamp of sectarianism,' foreshadowed in its religious life the variety and lay activism which were later to become characteristic of the whole American religious scene.[29]

In contrast with the period of the colonial state churches, Littell claims that the Protestant churches now are uneasy because they tend to assume the validity of prior historical conditions in a time which no longer is controlled by them. He says, for example:

When Methodist or Baptist churches—for example—pass pious resolutions on public issues, resolutions which have no binding authority on their own members or no real influence in public life, they are guilty of . . . self-righteousness of tone and presumptuousness of judgment. . . .

Those who act in this way are

. . . disclosing the mind-set of once dominant Protestant bodies grown accustomed to speaking for the majority and continuing to talk the same way after they have ceased to have the constituents or the moral authority so to do. The society has become pluralistic: The Jews and the Catholics are there, and other Protestant bodies. Their own members no longer follow with discipline: statistical success has been bought at the price of lowered entrance and membership standards.[30]

To Littell, a protagonist of the present, "the situation of religious voluntaryism and pluralism in which the American Protestants now find themselves, understood historically, is a positive good—both theologically and politically." [31] Despite his earnest overstatements, Littell points clearly to the fact that over the decades the Protestant churches in America have undergone significant historical movement in both their relations to the state and their own conception of themselves.

The historical movement from "state church to pluralism" is only one of the significant historical changes that have occurred within American history (and at other times and places) that show the church as a social institution in its dynamic character.

The new cultural atmosphere of "pluralism" has been accompanied by a new spirit of self-examination and even criticism on the part of some churches. Thus, Andrew M. Greeley and Peter H. Rossi recently completed an objective report, using a fairly large national sample of adults and teen-agers, of the education of Catholic Americans. Making comparisons among those with an all-Catholic, those with some Catholic, those with no Catholic education—along with a great many variables under such broad headings as participation in church life, breadth of religious knowledge, doctrinal orthodoxy, attitudes toward social issues, educational and occupational success—the investigators draw valuable conclusions regarding the effectiveness of parochial versus public education. They conclude, among other things, that Catholic schools are not in themselves divisive factors in American life, that Catholic education and a Catholic family tradition are mutually reinforcing, that Catholic schools have not been necessary for the survival of American Catholicism, and that lack of exposure of Catholics to Catholic education does not lead to a notable decline in at least minimal allegiance.[32] Such efforts and objectivity have tended in recent years to supplant former imperialistic and defensive claims of religious bodies.

The three significant changes (mobility on the church-sect continuum, secularization, and historical movement) illustrate the dangers inherent in any conception of the church as a static social institution. No classification, even the cleverest, can do full justice to the complexity of the church as a social institution.

3

Changing Perspectives:
The State

THE FAILURE OF TRADITION

The societies of the whole world, not just the West, may in the present era be faced with such fateful challenge to their political assumptions as to call for the most vigorous intellectual response. Many witnesses have testified to this fact. Karl Polanyi, for example, has addressed himself to the historical dimensions of the disintegration and collapse of nineteenth-century liberal civilization. He describes the historical significance of the "self-regulating market" and its consequences in the building of Western capitalism. He also is profoundly aware of the failure of the "self-regulating market" in the face of the threats, appeals, and pressures of twentieth-century living.

Polanyi calls for the rediscovery of the importance of society in contrast with the autonomy of privately held values. He also sees the need for a fresh and massive re-integration of economics and politics. He asserts that a "great transformation" has occurred within the relatively recent decades. This "transformation" calls fundamentally for a thoroughgoing re-examination of the political heritage.[1]

Reinhold Niebuhr similarly has written of the bankruptcy of historical liberalism. Niebuhr declares that twentieth-century man lives in a period of peril. On the one hand, his categories of traditional support for economic and political theory have become debilitated, frustrated, and unworkable. On the other hand, man in this period is faced with a variety of economic and political demonries that tend to rush into the vacuum left by the failure of tradition. These, such as fascism and Marxism, possess an inadequate understanding of the human situation and seek to apply inadequate solutions. The present circumstances, therefore, require that the philosophical assumption underlying the nature of the state be re-examined with care.[2]

It may be unsettling to some to face the complexity of religion in a realistic way, realizing that the church is a social institution among other social institutions, possessing an amazing diversity of forms which in themselves seem to defy inclusive categorization. It may be equally unsettling for others to face a political reality, the state, which also is a social institution among other social institutions, and which like the other social institutions is enormously complex and variable in its nature and expressions and which nowhere possesses the dictum of finality. Yet the state, like the church, can be understood adequately only when it is viewed from the standpoint of the diversity of its historical manifestations.

TWO PERSPECTIVES

The long and variable tradition concerning the nature and function of the state cannot be adequately reviewed here. But it is possible for the present purposes to assert that two important and persistent perspectives have existed.

The first claims an absolute legitimacy and autonomy for the state. The second asserts the liberal or empirical conception of the nature and function of the state. Obviously, to reduce the acknowledged complexity of the subject into two general categories is to oversimplify, but it is hoped that this conscious effort will achieve brevity and place the essential issues in review. Each of these tendencies will be summarized historically.

The Autonomous State

Plato (427?-347 B.C.) stands as a primary example in ancient times of the tradition which accords absolute legitimacy and autonomy to the state. His teachings are apparent in his attitude toward Democritus and in his exposition in the *Republic*.[3] Democritus (c. 460-c. 370 B.C.) advocated an atomistic philosophy of existence. Such a philosophy is readily adaptable to a democratic, empirical, or liberal view of the state. Democritus was opposed to all strong passions and convictions. He believed in the evolution of nature and social institutions. As a utilitarian of sorts, he was inclined to pragmatic solutions. While he believed in the propriety of slavery, he also favored freedom of speech and what now might be called democratic political expression. Plato, however, who lived about thirty years after Democritus, strongly resented Democritus' views. It is said that he even wished that Democritus' books be burned.

Plato's social philosophy stands in contradistinction to that of Democritus. In the *Republic* he espoused a social philosophy which gave support to those later political theorists who also asserted the absolute legitimacy and autonomy of the state. Plato was consciously committed to the development of a strong sense of nationalism. Although he did not analyze his justifications for this, he depended upon it as an assumption basic to his ideal state. Plato advocated a special brand of education, thought control, and censorship as a legitimate set of instrumentalities whereby the state as such could secure its autonomy. He was distrustful of the leadership of the masses, and advocated an oligarchic form of government in which a small, self-appointed group maintains its power by propaganda, lies, and violence if necessary. His lofty vision of the Idea and the Good was restricted to the few. He was opposed to empiricism and relativism by the very character of his aristocratic-conservative political theory.

In more recent times, the German philosopher Georg Hegel (1770-1831) gave expression to views similar to those of Plato. Probably Hegel was more extreme than Plato in his assertion of the nature of reality as an Absolute Idea. Like Plato, he found a foil for his resentments against empiricism—in John Locke (1632-1704), the founder of modern empiricism. Locke held that all knowledge is founded ultimately in experience rather than in abstract ideas. He was sympathetic to the principles of liberty, toleration, and self-government. Hegel, however, developed a philosophical system which was grounded upon absolutism. Perhaps it is not accidental, therefore, that modern totalitarian movements, such as fascism and communism, have been more receptive to the ideas of Hegel than of Locke. Hegel believed that the temporal and the abstract processes of history are developed in a highly logical process called the "dialectic." The goal of the dialectical process is the approximation to the final Reality. To prove his point, he attempted to show that various societies, including China, India, Greece, Rome and the Germanic, are set in a dialectical course of

universal development.[4] He strongly supported political
leaders of great vigor and even of totalitarian tendencies:
Alexander, Caesar, Napoleon. He firmly believed that an
autonomous state could properly exercise its unlimited
power to compel men to act for the best. Democracy, in
his opinion, lacked that strong central control and im-
petus by which societies could quickly and thoroughly
approximate to the Reality which to him was both a
personal and a universal obligation in history.

Thus, Hegel continued and implemented the general
view of Plato and others that the state possesses an absolute
legitimacy and autonomy. From this general standpoint,
the function of the state is not that of providing for the
general welfare; it is the function of the state to simply
enhance itself. The material needs of the members of the
political community are not intrinsically and systematically its concern. Similarly, the state in this view is not
bound by the moral and spiritual limitations which the
church may wish to impose upon it. Plato, Hegel, and
others laid the groundwork both for the development of
the uncontrolled and unlimited state in modern times
and for the growth of the philosophy and practice of
capitalistic *laissez-faire*.

The Empirical State

From ancient times, the absolutizing tendencies of certain thinkers in the political tradition have been opposed.
Plato had his Democritus; Hegel, his Locke. Those who
oppose the view that the state possesses an absolute legitimacy and autonomy are difficult to characterize, since their
presuppositions and conclusions vary greatly. The last centuries, however, have witnessed a decline in the Plato-
Hegel type of thinking about the state, with several nota-

ble exceptions, and a considerable development and acceptance of the empirical alternative.

One of the more able exponents of political empiricism in recent times is Bertrand Russell.[5] Russell's objections to the traditionally dominant view of the state take several forms.

First, he is opposed to the ideal of static perfection. He thinks that Plato, Hegel, and others were too enamored of the absolute. He detects that man is placed in an endless sea of change, but he does not confuse change with progress. "Change" to Russell is a scientific category, while "progress" is ethical. Change is a characteristic of reality, while progress is a matter of controversy. In his view, an adequate political philosophy of the state must be based upon the possibility of understanding change, of being receptive to it, and of seeking to control it by scientific methods.

Second, Russell believes that the first task of political theory, as of the state itself, is to steer clear of the extremes of despotism and anarchy. He asserts that Plato, Hegel and others followed the course of despotism. In his view, their teachings have led to great human misery. Yet he is well aware of the possible consequences of a genuine lack of a positive theory of the state. Thus, it is not enough to oppose despotism; perhaps in its place anarchism will come, unless vigorously intelligent ideas and actions are undertaken. The fundamental criterion of intelligent ideas and actions is the scientific method. This method, according to Russell, does not operate abstractly or even philosophically; it is skeptical of all systems, basing itself upon piecemeal empirical efforts.

Third, Russell, like other advocates of empiricism or liberalism, holds that the empirical alternative stands half-way between dogma and skepticism. He claims, as does Karl Polanyi, for example, that all absolutes have been dissolved in the present period. Knowledge, by its very nature, is in some degree doubtful. In the light of experience one theory gives way to another. Only a scientific temper, which accepts theories as useful hypotheses for research and correction, is permitted. Almost all hypotheses have some element of truth or virtue in them, but no intelligent person would regard any as immutably perfect.

From this standpoint, the nature and function of government, like everything else, are open to analysis and modification. The empirical viewpoint is highly amenable to pragmatic solutions and goals. To it, the question is not "What is the nature and function of the state?," but "What is it that men wish the state to do for them?" The state as such possesses no absolute legitimacy and autonomy. It does not exist to fulfill itself; it exists to answer the needs of people. The empirical conception of the state, therefore, looks with favor upon the innovations which governments in the more recent decades have made in their efforts to maximize the general welfare, meaning by the "general welfare" the material satisfactions of people as well as their personal and social freedoms and growth.

The views of the empirical tradition, however, are not always as salutary as Russell and others imagine. For example, if it is possible for the empirically conceived state to take positive action in the face of inevitable change, it is also possible for the state to take negative action. In ancient times, Protagoras (c. 481-411? B.C.) held an essentially skeptical or empirical view of reality, yet was essentially conservative in his political outlook. Similarly, David Hume (1711-1776) in modern times advocated a rather fierce skepticism in philosophy and even in scientific method, but his political sympathies were with the Tories. Another empiricist, Thomas Hobbes (1588-1679), although less skeptical than Hume, denied the divine origin of the state and concluded that an extreme conservatism or support of the *status quo* was desirable.

Also, the views of Russell and others are fallacious in that they imply that conviction and tolerance are incompatible. On this score, René de Visme Williamson argues to the contrary.[6] Williamson claims that belief in absolute values does not obligate the believer either by conscience or by logical necessity to impose such values on people who do not accept them; in fact, in a democratic state, the assumption is made that the state governs by consent rather than by force. Democracy is not opposed to absolute values and, indeed, for some may itself be just such a value.

The foregoing discussion aims, in a highly simplified manner, to show that historically several views have been held of the nature of the state.

Thus, the purpose of the foregoing discussion is not that of providing a comprehensively final analysis of the nature of the state as a social institution, but is basically an attempt to indicate in summary and historical fashion some of the complexities and ambiguities in thinking of the state as a social institution.

FORMS OF THE STATE

Although political scientists and others have long been in disagreement upon the nature of the state, they have been relatively in agreement regarding the several forms which the state historically has taken. The effort to delineate the forms of the state is similar to the effort to describe the forms of the church, as discussed in the previous chapter, although obviously the typologies differ both in method and in content. These differences should be anticipated, since church and state are social institutions which possess different functions socially and satisfy different individual needs.

The traditional classification of the forms of the state, generally agreed upon by political thinkers of widely differing theoretical assumptions, is threefold: (1) monarchy, (2) oligarchy, and (3) democracy. Herodotus, for example, relates an account of an argument that occurred between seven "magnates" of Persia in ancient times to whom it fell to determine a constitution for that country. These wise leaders concluded that the state could be a monarchy, an oligarchy, or a democracy. Each form of the state had its advocate, who was quick to point out the evils associated with the other two. Herodotus declares that the magnates decided for monarchy by a majority of one.[7]

Plato, that great political thinker of Greece, concluded in the eighth and ninth books of the *Republic* that there are only three essential forms of government: (1) monarchy, (2) oligarchy, and (3) democracy. He added, however, that each form of government has both a positive and a negative potential. Monarchy in its degenerate form is tyranny; aristocracy in its degenerate form is oligarchy, and democracy in its degenerate form turns into mobocracy. Upon review, Plato, like Herodotus, rated monarchy as the best, although he also admitted that its degenerate form of tyranny was the worst of all.[8]

In his *Politics,* Aristotle followed the lead of Plato in describing the forms of the state. He differs from Plato, though, in using the word "polity" to describe the constitutional "rule of the many," in which government is devoted to the interests of the whole, while "democracy" is a term which he reserves for the corrupt form. It well may be that Aristotle meant to differentiate by these two terms, "polity" and "democracy," those forms of government in which, respectively, there is the dominance of the middle classes and that of the lower classes.[9]

The tripartite classification of the nature of the state, with minor variations of language, has predominated almost all systems of classifying the nature of the state. Variations did occur, of course, as when Spinoza, for example, while adopting the whole Platonic arrangement, including Plato's three degenerate forms, expressed a preference for democracy.[10]

Also, there have been those who, while accepting the tripartite classification, have preferred some combination of the three. Cicero, for example, in his *De Republica* regarded "mixed governments" as the best.[11] Similarly, Thomas Aquinas thought that some combination of the three forms was desirable.[12]

The threefold analysis of the forms of the state, like Troeltsch's analysis of "church" and "sect," is probably categorically correct, but also needs even more precise analysis. Other criteria than the constitutional need to be applied. A feudal state, for example, possesses an economic structure quite different from that of a capitalistic state. So also a city-state differs geographically from a nation-state. The federated, socialistic dictatorship of the Soviet Union is quite different historically from the multi-country empire which constituted the Austro-Hungarian Empire. Again, the political form in Great Britain is one thing, while that of the British Commonwealth is another. The theocracy of the ancient Jews is different morally from the government of the Nazi period of modern Germany.

Walt Rostow, in a widely read work, has sought to

develop a new version of the old formulation of economic determinism. He seeks to tie the form of the state to the form of the economy, making political expressions the necessary epiphenomena of economic developments. To him "there is a direct causal relationship between the stage of economic development and politics." [13] On the basis of this thesis some have argued, for example, that the Soviet Union and the United States are inevitably becoming similar in political forms, since both feature highly industrialized economies. This notion has widespread acceptance.

But the assumption is false; its formulation is too general and sweeping. Moreover, it could be turned on its head (political forms determine economic forms) and possess the same degree of cogency. In this connection, the recent study by two experts on the Soviet Union provides a desired corrective. Professors Zbigniew Brzezinski and Samuel P. Huntington seek to answer three basic questions in comparing the political systems of the Soviet Union and the United States: (1) What are the principal similarities and dissimilarities between these systems? (2) What are the strengths and weaknesses of each system? (3) Are the two systems becoming more or less alike? Their response to the last question is of interest here. They conclude that it is not possible to claim that the two systems are becoming alike. They point ". . . to many examples which suggest that industrial complexity and maturity do not necessarily cause political uniformity and moderation. Essen under the Nazis was similar to Detroit in an economic and technological, as well as a cultural, sense, yet the similarity did not preclude the Nazis from imposing on the society a relationship of mobilization and control quite unlike the one prevailing in Detroit." [14] The lesson to be drawn seems to be: don't marry any two social factors, such as economics and politics, into a necessary, universal, and exclusive contract.

In small and great ways, the tripartite classification of the forms of the state needs further elucidation. The three forms, like "church" and "sect," should be considered as "ideal types," rather than the precise equivalents of any historical expression of the state. Efforts to establish an adequate subclassification of the three primal forms of the state, such as that attempted by Robert MacIver, seem never quite able to snare the elusive facts of history into a neatly compartmentalized paradigm.[15]

THE CHANGING STATE

The state as a social institution possesses many of the same attributes and processes that characterize the other social institutions, including the church. Many, if not all, of the themes developed in the previous chapter regarding the church as a social institution (and others, too) hold true for the state. For example, the social institution of the state is not a static reality. It changes as the other social institutions do. Plato recognized the dynamic character of the state, holding that each form of the state generates a succeeding form and that the over-all process is downward or negative.[16] The process, however, was held to be self-renewing, in that the establishment of the worst forms of government led naturally to efforts to achieve their opposites.

Similarly, the rise of the nation-state covers several centuries and involves a variety of cultural changes. For example, the rise of the nation-state probably would have been impossible without the liberating economic and technical developments of modern civilization. Closely related to its growth have been the rise and the decline of the empire-state. In the early stages of the nation-state the inherent dynamics of nationalism and the broad territorial realities in the world gave rise to an expansionist definition of the nation. This pan-national phenomenon is illustrated by the old-line empires: Spanish, Portuguese, German, British. It also found its expression in Europe, for example, in federations of countries, such as the Austro-Hungarian Empire.

The nation-state movement, however, which at one time favored the growth of the empire-state, later became modified in form as the recession of empire occurred. The dynamics of the state in the period following the Second World War favored the recession of empire and the outbreak in all parts of the world of strongly focused nation-states. Such states today predominantly define the nature of nationalism and, therefore, of the nation-state.

The nation-state, then, has not been a static reality, but has grown and expressed itself in a variety of forms. The state, as this discussion has tried to show, is responsive to influences from beyond itself. Like every social institution, the state is characterized by changeability.

INTERACTIONISM

All social institutions possess a somewhat paradoxical existence. They are formed for the maintenance of particular social functions, yet each overlaps the others and to some degree must be integrated with every other in order that society maintain its coherence and efficiency. Church and state are both related and unrelated to each other. Although at certain points the church is in conflict with the state, in other ways it is highly related to the state's functioning. When the church, in the promotion of its own values, urges legislation on gambling, education, political corruption, racial discrimination, divorce, child labor, foreign relations, liquor consumption, and other matters, it has moved within the circle of the functions of the state. The church, moreover, is not necessarily always in agreement with itself. One denomination may consent to action on the part of the state, while another may actively oppose it. In the case of Negro slavery in the United States, the churches in the North and in the South strongly supported the views and actions of their respective governments.

On some issues effecting church and state relations, divergent views are held both among the several churches and within the general citizenry. Thus, in June, 1962, the United States Supreme Court held that the action of a local school board in the state of New York in providing for the daily recitation by children of the nonsectarian prayer recommended by the Board of Regents was unconstitutional. Although children were free not to participate in the recitation of this prayer, the Supreme Court held that the practice was nevertheless invalid since it constituted the establishment of religion in violation of the First Amendment to the Constitution. Somewhat later the Supreme Court decided two other cases dealing with religious practices in public schools. In these cases the Court held that the recitation of the Lord's Prayer and the reading of a chapter or a certain number of verses of the Bible without comment at the beginning of the school day were also unconstitutional when required by state law. The Court viewed the practice of reading the Bible without comment as a religious practice which was, therefore, unconstitutional on the same basis that it had made its judgment on the prayer cases. The consequences, within the churches and without, were mixed. Some churches were highly critical of the Supreme Court, while others praised the Court for freeing religion from public compulsion. A similar divergence of opinion was expressed among some legislators. One consequence, for example, was the effort of Senator Everett Dirksen and others to secure an amendment to the Constitution permitting religious practices in the schools.[17]

Similarly, the state does not function in isolation from the church. Rather, at certain points the state acts in a manner that overtly or inferentially provides support to the church. The government of the United States, for example, regularly operates within the circle of functions commonly ascribed to the church when it supports chaplains in Congress, the Armed Forces, and correctional and other institutions, when it exempts religious contributions from taxable income, reduces postal rates for religious publications, makes church property tax-exempt and, among other things, assists foreign missionaries in their work as citizens of the United States.

But, despite the interaction that always exists between social institutions in a society, the claim cannot be made that one institution is utterly dependent upon the other. Some form of the church may always be interacting with some form of the state, but no specific form of either is necessary for the maintenance of the interrelationship. In fact, the history of Western civilization is replete with examples in which many diverse forms of church and state have been at different times both cooperative and hostile.

At times, these relations between church and state are highly complicated. Thus, Poland's millennium in 1966, the anniversary of the nation's conversion to Christianity, was as much a quarrel as it was a celebration. The squabble continues. Early in 1967 Stefan Cardinal Wyszynski was once again at loggerheads with the tough secular party boss, Wladyslaw Gomulka. This time the issue was state regulation of seminaries. The Cardinal ordered the doors to some of the Roman Catholic seminaries closed to inspectors sent by the government to supervise the government decree that its authority extends not only to supervision of nonreligious subjects taught in the seminaries but to appointment of teachers and the regulation of enrollments as well. Gomulka's rude veto of a papal visit during the millennium illustrates the tenacity of the state, but no one expects that the rugged old Cardinal will stop his verbal assaults on the attempted domination of the church by the state.

The existence of the church as a social institution does not depend directly upon the existence of the state, and vice versa. The Protestant Raymond C. Knox summarized this understanding: "Christianity, as it cannot too strongly be stated, is not committed to any political system or form of government." [18] Roman Catholic Archbishop John Ireland emphasized the same point: "The Church is at home under all forms of government. . . ." [19]

INHERENT PRETENSE

Although all social institutions enjoy a high degree of cooperative interaction, they also are capable of disharmony and conflict. The social institutions may be arranged or ordered in scalar form according to the intensity of their comprehensive claim to control the behavior of people. Some social institutions—perhaps the family, education, and recreation, for example—seem to have a low pretense toward inclusiveness. These social institutions do not appear to need a high degree of systematically developed and socially managed ideological support for their efficiency. The recreational interests in the United States, for instance, are not organized in such a way that every citizen feels it an obligation to be a participant in some form of organized recreation. The family system of the United States is not organized to advocate itself and its ultimate claim upon the lives of every individual. These institutions of low pretense, despite their great success, are marked by a lack of "imperialistic" claims.

In the middle range of inherent pretense to inclusiveness stands such a social institution as the economy. In part the economy is characterized by highly organized associations that make pretentious claims for its ultimacy in relation to the lives of every individual. Such claims are often apparent, for example, when comparisons are made of the economies of the United States and the Soviet Union.

Both the church and the state exert a high pretense toward inclusiveness. These social institutions for the most part cannot be content to hold the loyalties of only a part of the total population. Their ideational and symbolic bases rest upon suprarational factors, the highest and most abstract element of which is God or Providence. Sometimes the inclusive claims of the social institutions of church and state, based upon the idea of Providence, are conjoined in mutuality, as Perry Miller shows for a history of Virginia which begins with Adam and Eve in order to "show how God had so managed the past that English colonization in the present was the fulfillment of His plan." [20] At other times, however, the pretense to inclusiveness has involved a concentration upon competition for power, as J. Milton Yinger shows in his historical study of the relationships between religious organizations and political regimes that were concerned fundamentally with establishing and maintaining their exclusive influence over human beings.[21]

A study by the Center for the Study of Democratic Institutions has put the problem of the convergence and divergence of church and state as all-inclusive social institutions into the language of the present. This study claims that there is a case to be made both for and against a "public philosophy" or a "consensus." Those who took part in the study (William Clancy, John Cogley, Arthur A. Cohen, Robert Gordis, William Gorman, F. Ernest Johnson, Robert Lekachman, and William Lee Miller) state the dilemma they faced in their study:

Some Americans who speak about the necessity for a public philosophy, a consensus, or who accent the words of the Declaration, 'we hold these truths . . . ,' are enthusiastic about the development. But the discussion has not been universally hailed. Other Americans, representing a large and significant school of thought, have felt that the whole idea of spelling out a national purpose is foreign to the American genius, which they regard as strongly pragmatic and dependent for its continued vitality on a live-and-let-live spirit. The very articulation of a 'purpose,' they hold, is alien to our tradition.[22]

Both schools of thought were represented in the group signing the statement.

Those who believe that a social and moral consensus, no matter by what term they may call it, is both possible and desirable tend to minimize the possibility and presence of conflict between the social institutions of church and state. They look to a doctrine of Providence, a trust in man's rationality, a philosophic doctrine of "natural law," or to some other support by which their position is maintained.

Those who believe that a public philosophy or consensus is not possible and is actually undesirable tend to be skeptical of the scholastic understanding of "truth" as a conformity of intellect to objective reality; they fear the danger to a free society of those convinced that they hold the truth, and look upon the tensions and conflicts that exist among competing groups as capable of producing a positive good for the whole of society.

The first group, through one expression or another, tends to believe that the social institutions of church and state are complementary and that they function best when they emphasize their mutuality of goals or even the identity of their overarching purposes. The second group is inclined to accept the inevitable separation of church and state and the ever-present possibility of the institutions' being in conflict with each other, although it is assumed by some who hold the latter position that even this conflict is for the greater glory of man, society, and God.

4

Church-State in the Bible

The appeal to the Bible in support of previously drawn
positions is now so well known as fallacious as to require
no extended comment. There may be some who utilize
the Bible to "proof-text" the subject of church and state
in a self-conscious way, but probably they are few. Even
in those instances where the accusation is a temptation, it
is probably fair to say that a more complex process than
that of consciousness alone has entered into the arrangement. And, in fact, it is clear that there are many who
seek in a learned and objective way not to fit the Bible
to their prejudices, but to explore it for its ancient and
current relevancy. It is in this latter spirit that a review
of the Bible's teaching on church and state is appropriate.

Such a review runs the danger of Biblicism. This idea
assumes the validity and necessary conditioning today
of any and all ideas that are found in the Bible, as though
the Bible has a simple, direct, and compelling control over
those who accept its authority. The noted theologian Archbishop William Temple said on this score: "The revelation
is received in a living experience; all doctrines are in-

ferences drawn from that revelation in the context provided by the rest of experience; and their spiritual value
is not in themselves; it is in the directions which they offer
for recovering the experience from which they spring." [1]

The application of Archbishop Temple's understanding
is illustrated in the work of the Special Committee on
Church and State of the United Presbyterian Church in
the United States of America when it states:

"Render to Caesar the things that are Caesar's and to God
the things that are God's" is a quotation often applied to
church-state relations. This quote *does not* have direct application to the series of problems before our Church! The
New Testament denies such application. The issue before
the Church is not "What is Caesar's and what is God's."
Caesar has no autonomy over against God whether he knows
it or not! The issue is, what does it mean to follow a Lord
who, when confronted with a double-edged question, silenced
his antagonists with a double-edged answer? We cannot concern ourselves with the legalistic question of what is God's
and what is Caesar's. This is beside the point. Our job is to
follow Christ and in so doing enter into the life-filled task
of demonstrating that the will of God is good, acceptable, and
perfect.[2]

A review of the often conflicting, developmental, yet
significant concepts of church and state in the Bible may
provide needed understanding of these terms, an appreciation of the historical interpretations that have been drawn
(to be discussed in some detail in the next two chapters),
and a safeguard against literalistic simplicity.

FOUR METHODS

A Biblical review, despite its complex and difficult requirements, is simply one approach to an understanding from within the Christian faith of the nature of the church and the state and their relationships. A more complete catalogue of methods, including the Biblical, would include (1) the Biblical, (2) the historical, (3) the sociological, and (4) the theological. Each of the four utilizes its own starting point for an understanding of the subject, yet each is incomplete without reference to the other. In fact, in extended discussions each approach necessarily involves the others. These four will be discussed briefly.

Biblical

The Biblical approach may be based upon several interests. First, the Biblical account may be analyzed from a descriptive standpoint. Since the Bible contains many references to concrete aspects of church and state, it may be studied factually. This method seeks primarily to describe and perhaps to categorize the manifold events of the Scriptural traditions so far as they pertain to the subject under discussion. Second, the Biblical approach also may be employed to establish normative standards for the relations between the several areas of society. Such a method may employ descriptive materials from the Bible, but commonly it arranges them in ways that give support to transcendent principles. Both Biblical approaches, moreover, have been employed in combination.

Historical

The historical approach may depend in part upon Biblical analysis, but it also may be focused upon other aspects of the long course of the development of the Christian churches and their interaction with the other social institutions in society. The historical method may concentrate primarily upon the relationships between the churches and the political orders in a particular nation or nations (such as western Europe).[3] It may be centered upon the development of the relationships in a given period of time and within a particular nation.[4] Similarly, the historical approach may be concerned primarily with the dynamic interrelationships between an aspect of the Christian faith and an aspect of the social order.[5] Other kinds of historical investigation also are available. The historical approach, however, is primarily descriptive, and only on occasion seeks to go beyond the recounting of past events and relationships to the formulation of normative standards.

Sociological

The sociological approach is illustrated by the discussion of the nature of social institutions in Chapter 1 of this book, although other types of sociological investigation may be employed. The sociological point of view regards such entities as church and state as thoroughly human forms that are amenable to social science analysis. Happily, an increasing number of sociologists and others, notwithstanding their personal convictions regarding religion, are expanding available knowledge through that subdiscipline called "the sociology of religion." [6]

A particularly sound and useful treatise on the church from a sociological viewpoint has been provided by James M. Gustafson, who discusses the church as a human community, a natural community, a political community, a community of language, a community of interpretation, a community of memory and understanding, and a community of belief and action. Gustafson, in speaking of the church as a natural community, says:

The reference is to the communal life of Christian people wherever and whenever they gather as Christians. Thus it refers to a local congregation, a denomination, or a council of churches. It refers to the sense of being one people that Christians have as a global religious community, even though this community never meets as a whole.[7]

As a sociologist and as a theologian, Gustafson is able to see merit in the functional theory of the relevance of social institutions as the means whereby human needs are satisfied. In speaking of the church as a natural community, he states:

Certain human needs can be met at each social level. For example, most human beings need to have their personal values sustained and confirmed by others; they need to participate in a community that has a common outlook on life and the world. Personal values can be nourished in the meeting of a congregation, in a general assembly of a denomination, in a conference meeting for a weekend, or in a meeting of an international Christian group. One person may have this need met better in a small prayer group in a local congregation, another in a mass assembly. The Church fulfills certain

needs more adequately in one social form than in another.
. . . But whenever the Church is gathered some of man's
natural needs are met.[8]

Theological

The theological approach utilizes a wide variety of
materials for its investigations. Biblical, historical, and
sociological studies provide grist for the theological mill,
but the theological method also operates on its own
principles. Theological analyses may be primarily descriptive, but generally they seek to be normative. They tend
to view existential problems in the light of essential solutions.[9]

The utilization of these several approaches, and others,
does not lead to a preordained harmony of views. In part
they may be employed as complements to each other, but
in part, since they are based upon specialized methods and
language, they make apparent the discontinuities in the
general understanding of the phenomena studied. Gustafson stresses the problem of the discontinuities when he
asks the following questions:

How can the same phenomenon, the Church, be understood
from two radically diverse perspectives? Does the use of
doctrinal language require inherently the exclusion of the
language of social thought? Does a social interpretation of the
Church necessarily exclude the more distinctively theological
and doctrinal interpretation? If the two are not mutually exclusive, how can the significance of the social processes and
elements be theologically understood? [10]

Mindful of the limitations previously discussed, the
Biblical review of the church and the state, now to be
undertaken, will be restricted chiefly to descriptive ac-

counts. Despite this primary limit, however, elements of the other approaches undoubtedly will be either apparent or inferable.

THE CHURCH
IN THE OLD TESTAMENT

The church in the New Testament is the reconstitution of the Old Testament people of God, Israel, as God's people intended for mission. The historic roots of the church, then, are to be found in the Old Testament idea of a covenanted and chosen people.

The early church was well aware of its relationship to the chosen people of God. The writer to the Hebrews speaks of the new covenant which brought the church into existence as being a covenant with the "house of Israel." [11] Such a concept was held also by Paul, who called Christians "the true circumcision," [12] "the children of Abraham," [13] "the commonwealth of Israel." [14] Once he deliberately called them "the Israel of God." [15] Peter faithfully applied Old Testament descriptions of Israel to the newly founded church, calling Christians the "exiles of the Dispersion." [16] Jesus apparently was aware of the same heritage when he gave Israel's creed as the injunction to his followers: "Hear, O Israel: The Lord our God, the Lord is one; and you shall love the Lord your God with all your heart, and with all your soul, and with all your mind, and with all your strength." [17]

The covenant with Israel was established through Moses on Mount Sinai in the following declaration: "Now therefore, if you will obey my voice and keep my covenant, you shall be my own possession among all people; for the

earth is mine, and you shall be to me a kingdom of priests
and a holy nation." [18] This relationship freed Israel from
bondage and offered them their salvation. The people of
Israel, in turn, agreed to serve God's holy and sovereign
purpose.

According to the Old Testament, God established his
covenant with Israel alone, although his sovereignty extended over every nation. Israel has a special function in
the fulfillment of God's will for all nations, but as the Old
Testament repeatedly declares, God rules over all the
nations.

> All the ends of the earth shall remember
>   and turn to the Lord;
> and all the families of the nations
>   shall worship before Him.
> For dominion belongs to the Lord,
>   and He rules over the nations.[19]

God is not the exclusive possession of Israel. His covenant
with Israel is for the achievement of a universal purpose:

> I am the Lord, I have called you in righteousness,
>   I have taken you by the hand and kept you;
> I have given you as a covenant to the people,
>   a light to the nations,
>   to open the eyes that are blind,
>   to bring out the prisoners from the dungeon,
>   from the prison those who sit in darkness.[20]

The covenant with Israel related to the corporate
responsibility of the people. The covenant established a
community in which exemplary individual behavior was
required. The Ten Commandments, with their elaboration
to specific aspects of behavior, became the norm for indi-

vidual conduct.[21] But the covenant referred to the fact
that religion and corporate life were bound in a unique
way. Israel was one, and the behavior of each individual
was considered to be intimately related to the welfare of
the group as a whole. The story of Achan illustrates this
point. The destruction of Jericho led to the capturing of
booty which was to be "devoted" to God. "Devotion"
meant that none of the booty was to be kept, but all of
it was to be destroyed as an offering to God. But Achan
disobeyed and "took some of the devoted things." By this
act, Achan sinned indeed, but the Biblical writer felt that
"the people of Israel broke faith in regard to the devoted
things; for Achan . . . took some . . . and the anger of
the Lord burned against the people of Israel." [22] So, it
seems, the action of any individual is related to the
corporate nature of the nation in its relation to God and
his covenant.

Again, the covenant between God and Israel, in the Old
Testament view, is not to be understood on the basis of
the size of the covenanted people, their goodness, or their
uncommon ability: "It was not because you were more in
number than any other people that the Lord sent his love
upon you and chose you, for you were the fewest of all
peoples, but it is because the Lord loves you." [23] It was
the nature of God's love which called Israel into a covenanted relationship, rather than any virtue on the part of
the people themselves. As Jeremiah put it: "I have loved
you with an everlasting love; therefore I have continued
my faithfulness to you." [24]

God's love was the basis for the covenant with Israel,
but the presumed response of Israel was that of obedience
—obedience to the ethical will of God. Said Jeremiah:

"Listen to my voice, and do all that I command you. So shall you be my people, and I will be your God." [25] Israel's response was clear: "All that the Lord has spoken we will do, and we will be obedient." [26] But Israel repeatedly misunderstood and broke its covenant. It considered the covenant as a mark of special privilege. It disobeyed the requirements of God both within the nation and toward the nations of the world. The sinful nation was called to judgment through many "mighty acts" by God. This judgment, it was hoped, would lead to repentance and renewed faithfulness to the terms of the covenant, but the unfaithfulness continued and the idea of Israel being the special people of God became tempered in the teachings of Elijah, Amos, Micah, Jeremiah, Isaiah, and others in the message that God had turned his back upon Israel as a nation.

Henceforth he would maintain his covenant with a small and loyal community within the nation, a group to be called "the remnant." This idea was persistently applied throughout the exilic and postexilic periods (through the exiles in Babylonia and elsewhere).[27] It was also applied to the little postexilic community in Palestine.[28] God needed to make a new covenant.[29]

Christians consider the church to be at least one basis for this new covenant. The "new covenant" was conceived to be new not merely in the sense of being another. It would not be "like the covenant which I made with their fathers when I took them by the hand to bring them out of the land of Egypt." [30] The "new covenant" was to be written "upon their hearts." [31] This new covenant involved an inward transformation on the part of the people of Israel; it would be a "new exodus," a deliverance from a bondage greater even than that of Egypt. It would include all repentant persons who sought to live in covenant relations with God and who, by their relationships, would bring into being a new people of God. "I will be their God, and they shall be my people." [32]

THE CHURCH
IN THE NEW TESTAMENT

The English word "church" comes from the Greek word *kyriakon,* meaning "that which belongs to the Lord." This Greek word, however, is used only twice in the New Testament. Once it designates the Lord's Supper,[33] and once it is used in reference to the Lord's Day.[34] The English word "church," however, is used 115 times in the New Testament to translate the Greek word *ecclesia.* From this word "ecclesiastical" and similar words are derived. It signifies "the people called out" or the "people who belong to the Lord." In addition, there are other references in the New Testament to "the people who belong to the Lord" where *kyriakon* and *ecclesia* are not specifically employed. Commonly, in the usage of the times of the New Testament, *ecclesia* is used to refer to any public assembly of people called for any reason. The New Testament, however, does not speak of a calling out of people, but *the* calling out of people for the assembly. Thus, the New Testament speaks not of *a* church, but *the* church.

The church, moreover, consisted not only of those who had been called out of society to form a new body, but a group called to new relationships or to a new covenant with God in Jesus the Christ. So Paul, in writing to the

Christians at Corinth, said that they were "the church of God" because they were "sanctified in Christ Jesus" and called "on the name of our Lord Jesus Christ." [35] To the Christians at Ephesus, Paul wrote that they were "the church of the Lord which he obtained with his own blood." [36] From these and similar references, it is assumed that the church is that body of believers that has been called out of the general society to bear a new covenant relationship with God through their recognition of Jesus as the Christ.

The New Testament employs a number of terms to explain and enrich the idea of the church. The conception of the church as the bride of Christ, for example, is suggested in II Corinthians 11:2 and appears quite explicitly in Ephesians 5:22-33 and Revelation 19:7; 21:2, 9; 22:17. At other times individual churches are referred to as "elect sister." [37] A more frequent term for the church is "God's temple" or "God's house." [38] This term may be based upon the idea in the Old Testament that the temple —and the tabernacle before it—was the place where God dwelt in the midst of his people. It was in that place that God was worshiped and his presence felt. Since the old temple had been destroyed, the church became God's new dwelling place with his specially covenanted people.

The church in the New Testament is frequently called "the body of Christ." [39] Paul regularly uses the term "the body of Christ" to illustrate the unity in diversity of the church.

Another New Testament term for the church is the "household" or "family" of God. Thus, Jesus declared that all who believed were in a common family; they were his brothers, sisters, mother.[40] To be a Christian, in this view, meant that one had brotherly or familial relationships with those who were conjoined in the family of faith. The spiritual family relationship was considered more basic to life than that of earthly kinship. Jesus even spoke of the possibility that one might have to forsake "brothers or sisters or mother or father or children" for his sake.[41] The family of God, in the New Testament view, knew no boundaries of class, race, nation, or any other natural barrier. All men who by faith accepted the new covenant of God, as exemplified in Jesus as the Christ, were to be brought together in a universal brotherhood.

Consciousness of the church was fairly well developed by the time Matthew wrote his life of Jesus. The Greek word *ecclesia* is found only in his Gospel. Matthew shows his interest in the problems of membership and discipline in the early church through his telling of the parables of the tares and the dragnet in which, apparently, the presence of unworthy members in the church is recognized.[42] Also, the inclusion of the man without a wedding garment in the parable of the great supper provides a similar recognition.[43] It is in Matthew's Gospel, moreover, that the story of the building of the foundations of the church of Peter, to whom is given the power of admission and exclusion, is made available.[44] The idea that disputes among the members of the church should be referred to the church also is proposed by Matthew.[45]

In the later-written parts of the New Testament, the idea of the church is further developed. In Revelation, for example, the idea of Israel as a kingdom of priests is applied to the church.[46] Peter also includes this idea.[47] Hebrews teaches the idea of the new covenant's superseding the old to the point that it is quite clear that the church has taken the place of Israel itself. The discussion of the qualification of church officials, finally, brings the New Testament practically to the historical point where non-New Testament sources pick up.[48]

The previous description of the church, although brief and admittedly superficial, contains some descriptive formulations of the manner in which a Biblical review provides understanding of the nature of the church. Although church and state are closely connected in the Bible, they are being reviewed here separately in an effort to delineate their special characteristics, both historically and conceptually. Like the idea of the church, the state is expressed in the Bible in a complex but traceable way. A brief Biblical review of the nature of the state will now be attempted.

THE STATE
IN THE OLD TESTAMENT

The Old Testament provides a variety of conceptions of the nature of the state. There is no evidence that early Hebrew society featured a hereditary nobility or royalty. The clan and tribe in that early period were led by patriarchal guardians.[49] In time the tribes were united and given a sense of cohesion through the leadership of Moses. This leadership rested publicly upon divine sanction, and its success may have been due in no small part to the crisis facing the tribes in the wilderness. The fact that the patriarchal and the natural leadership of Moses was inadequate to the complexities of Hebrew society is supported by the story of the appointment of rulers of thousands, rulers of hundreds, rulers of fifties, and rulers of tens.[50] The Hebrew nation as such, however, originated as a consequence of the federation of the separate clans and tribes. They were bound by a covenant with God. This covenant was not the social contract of Rousseau; it was promulgated by the political leadership. A divine-human agreement, the covenant called for the active support of the people.[51] It may be that the covenant was not once and for all accepted by the Hebrew people, but that they annually pledged themselves anew to it.

The unified Hebrew nation developed two kinds of political leadership. First, within the city, which was the main form of communal life, government was in the hands of the elders of the city.[52] Local magistrates, whether appointed or elected, also held power.[53]

Second, Moses and Joshua were the first national leaders in Hebrew society. Later the judges were important officials (the word "judge" means "one who establishes justice"). These heroes, as the book of Judges illustrates, were not merely magistrates who conducted courts, although some judges did only this. The judges also were warriors who protected the citizens from oppression and punished the oppressors. The judges, however, did not act solely as agents of society. They also were the instruments of God, and all of their achievements were attributed to his will.[54] The judge, however, also had the responsibility of judging Israel even as Moses formerly had done.[55] Samuel, as well as Deborah, maintained the Mosaic tradition of leadership.[56]

Hebrew society, contrary to its earliest phases, gradually developed a monarch.[57] Probably the monarchy originated in a military crisis. The government of Saul, however, differed only on minor points from that of the earlier judges. David was apparently influenced by the political experience of the nations surrounding Israel, for the tendency toward the autonomy of the monarchy is clearly apparent in his reign. Solomon extended the power of the monarchy by establishing administrative districts that did not follow the old tribal frontiers. But even under Solomon the power of the state as expressed in the king was limited by his subjection to the will of God and by the governance of the people by the written law.[58]

The destruction of the kingdoms of Israel and Judah and the resulting Babylonian exile drastically changed the pattern of political development for the Jews: they became subject to foreign rulers. But even in this period they maintained a degree of control over their own civil affairs. Under these circumstances the high priests became in certain instances the leaders of the political community. It was possible, moreover, as in the case of Nehemiah, for the Jews to be ruled by a Jewish governor. Even in the New Testament, Herod and his sons ruled on the authority of Rome, and the religious authorities were recognized in such matters as were covered by the Jewish law.

The political organization of Jewish society in Old Testament times clearly was not democratic, yet the state was not viewed, as it was by Plato and Hegel, as a self-legitimizing and autonomous structure in society. The state secured its legitimacy in part from the covenanted relationship engaged in by the people themselves. But to a greater degree the state secured its support both through the acknowledgment of God and through God's placing of responsibility upon a variety of political forms and persons. The responsibility of government, however, is closely related to the welfare of the people. Both God and the political leaders were concerned with the welfare of the people. For example, David, in estimating his legitimacy as a ruler, declared that he acknowledged the fact that God had established him as king "for his people Israel's sake." [59] Similarly, the dominant contribution of the prophets was their championship of the common people and their belief that the people and the rulers alike were responsible to God for the common welfare.

Hebrew society, moreover, regularly assumed the right of revolution. Revolution was considered a proper recourse when the king violated the will of God.[60] Also, the right of revolution was asserted when the king became unacceptable to the people.[61] The right to revolution and self-determination was expressed by the northern tribes when they seceded from the kingdom of Rehoboam.[62] Again, the Old Testament contains one account of a Hebrew prophet instigating a revolution in another nation.[63] Such sentiment and action against the evils of autocratic political rule is reflected in Jesus' statement to the effect that his disciples must not lord it over one another as the rulers of the nations did.[64]

Yet the first recourse of a disgruntled citizen in Hebrew society was not that of revolution. Each individual held a responsibility to maintain the common good. In addition, the citizen held a responsibility for the correction and improvement of civil matters, as is illustrated in Jotham's fable.[65]

Religious and political institutions are intertwined throughout the Old Testament. No "wall of separation" characterized them. Jerusalem, for example, in the reign of David was both the political and the religious capital of the nation. He brought the ark there and made his own sons priests. Solomon built the temple. Both ruler and people bore a covenanted relationship to God and to Judaism as the cultus by which the whole society was bound. Even the division of the kingdom by Jeroboam and his adoption of the shrines of Dan and Bethel did not supplant Jerusalem as the symbol of the ultimately re-deemed community.

The monarchy tended to justify itself by reference to the theocratic ideal. At first the kings were able to justify their authority on the grounds simply that they possessed the spirit of God.[66] The king in that period was ceremonially granted his authority by being appointed in the name of God by a prophet.[67] Later the prophet's role was taken by the high priest.[68] Obviously, as in the instances of Saul and David, the choice of the monarch was assuredly popular.[69] With Solomon and his successors, heredity, with or without nomination by the predecessor, was the prime deter-minant of the choice of a ruler.[70] But, by whatever means the king was appointed and sanctified, he ruled as an agent both of God and the people. The monarchy was in fact a theocracy.

The acceptance of the Hebrew monarchy, however, was never easy or complete. Two attitudes toward the origin of the monarchy are found in 1 Samuel. They assume that God held two opposing views of its value. Similarly, Samuel and Saul found difficulty in gaining complete ac-ceptance by the people.[71] But later kings, who extended their autonomies far beyond those of the earlier kings, met the opposition of the prophets. The relations of Nathan and David, Ahijah and Solomon, and Elijah and Ahab reflect the prophetic opposition to the autonomous asser-tions of the later Hebrew monarchs.[72] Amos, Hosea,

Isaiah, Jeremiah, and Ezekiel all were bitterly critical of evil monarchs. The judgments of God on such political leaders, recounted in 1 and 2 Kings and chapters 44 to 46 of the book of Ezekiel, may well demonstrate the skepticism nourished by prior experience and applied to the role of the "prince" in the period of reconstruction.

THE STATE
IN THE NEW TESTAMENT

The New Testament is a much less rich source of information on the relationships of the holy people to the state than is the Old Testament.[73] Of course, the general political situation in New Testament times was markedly different. The period was one of great unrest, characterized by the Roman rule over a vassalized people. The New Testament period, so far as the relationships between the holy people and the state are concerned, was similar to that of the Jews in the period of exile. In both instances the people called of God suffered under the domination of alien political control. A primary possibility for Jesus and his followers in relation to the controlling Roman state was armed revolt. Such an option was not merely theoretical, as the revolt against Rome in A.D. 66-78 signifies. Yet Jesus apparently held a negative view on such efforts. He taught: "All who take the sword will perish by the sword."[74] Similarly, his temptation to bow to Satan and thereby gain the kingdoms of the world reveals his attitude on the matter.[75] Although one of his disciples was a Zealot, there is no recognition on his part of the validity of the cause of the Zealots.[76] Quite possibly Jesus was even critical of the position of the Zealots.[77]

The most quoted, and possibly the most relevant, verse in the Gospels on the attitude of Jesus toward the state is found in Mark 12:13-17, where Jesus stated: "Render to Caesar the things that are Caesar's; and to God the things that are God's." Obviously, however, this single statement, unrefined and undeveloped, constitutes an apt answer to a tricky question rather than a substantial explication of the relations of the Christian faith to the state. But it well may be that in this statement Jesus gave evidence of his recognition of the legitimacy of the state, even of a state which did not bear the stamp and spirit of the Christian sanction. More likely, he sought to affirm his sense of responsibility and concern for man's relation to God.

The early Christians suffered persecution by the state and by the Sanhedrin,[78] yet no highly developed and constructive doctrine of the relations of the Christian faith to the state developed as a result of this persecution. Paul, for example, was able to call upon his Roman citizenship as a hedge against the misuse of the powers of the state, although ultimately his appeal was not effective. His Roman citizenship provided him with an understandable basis for advocating the submission of the citizenry to the powers of the state.[79] At any rate, the dominance of his eschatological vision kept him from developing a systematic doctrine of the relations between church and state. Attitudes similar to that of Paul also can be found in the New Testament.[80] In fact, unreconciled advice is offered to those who are persecuted, as is evident in the contrast between 1 Peter 2:13-17 and 1 Peter 4:12-16.

Not until Revelation, when Rome was headed by the malevolent Nero, was a strong appraisal of the evil of the

Roman state asserted.[81] Rome is likened unto a great harlot which is drunk with the blood of the saints and martyrs.[82] But Revelation calls for no revolt against the evil power of Rome; it calls for loyalty to the faith and the passive acceptance of persecution.

Thus, the New Testament does not provide a systematic doctrine on the relations of church and state. Its attitude toward the state is fashioned by the particularities of given periods of human history in which the righteous people of God are set in opposition to the powers and dominations of the world. The New Testament provides little or no guidance to an understanding of a situation in which a marked degree of harmony of objectives exists between the religious views and ideals of the people and the responsible and humane exercise of state power. The welfare state, for example, has grown and exists in some societies in which the state does not view its citizens as hostile and alien to its purposes. In fact, the welfare state to some degree assumes the holding of power and the exercise of it by individuals and groups that are strongly influenced by the Christian faith. The New Testament experience is probably more relevant on the subject of the state to those modern nations where a notable cleavage exists between the rulers and the people, although even in such instances it is difficult to rely upon direct parallels from the New Testament social situation to the present time.

5

Church-State in Western History

GROWING SOPHISTICATION

The growing sophistication among religious leaders in the
United States, if not among laymen as well, on the subject
of church-state relations has led to an increased awareness
that a variety of relationships between church and state
are clearly possible and defensible. One might have supposed that such an awareness would be an inevitable consequence of an understanding of American history as well
as the history of Western civilization. Yet in the past there
has been a surprisingly naïve identification of the relations
of church and state with personal and denominational
viewpoints.

With the decline of the pan-Protestant era and the recognition of religious pluralism in the United States,
coupled with increased attention to the subject, the several
and diverse positions regarding church-state relations have
become increasingly evident. Sometimes this increased
awareness has led to the shriller and more aggressive presentation of particularistic views, but mostly it has led to
a state of growing toleration and understanding in which
the historical and current meanings of the diverse viewpoints are explored in an effort simply to understand the
diversity. As a consequence, a more pragmatic and piece-

meal approach to the understanding of church-state relations has begun to be the dominant mode of scholarly inquiry. John C. Bennett epitomizes the situation in this statement:

Recently I wrote a little book at the request of the International Missionary Council about Christian citizenship and I was supposed to make it applicable to all parts of the world, especially to the countries of the "younger churches" in Asia and Africa about which my knowledge is very limited. In my effort to carry out this assignment I came to realize how remote generalizations intended to apply to all situations are from many situations. I resolved then to write a book that would deal with some fullness with the problems in the United States with which I am most familiar.[1]

TYPOLOGIES

If the current tendency is toward specific or discrete studies of the relations of church and state, another tendency also is apparent. In part, the second tendency is required by the first. It is the effort to create a satisfying and inclusive typology of church-state relations. An adequate typology is seen as a requirement for the successful pursuit of discrete studies and, indeed, as a consequence of them. The appearance in recent years of a variety of efforts to create such typologies, moreover, has in itself tended to demonstrate to the uninitiated that the subject of church-state relations is indeed very complex.

Richard Niebuhr

Reference was made in Chapter 2 to the typological efforts of H. Richard Niebuhr, who, although from a

wider perspective, delineated five essential relationships
between "Christ and culture": (1) Christ against culture;
(2) the Christ of culture; (3) Christ above culture; (4)
Christ and culture in paradox; and (5) Christ the transformer of culture.[2] Niebuhr's typology is heavily weighted
with theological formulations taken from a wide variety of
historical sources. He is more concerned with the relations
of "Christ" to "culture" than he is with the relations of
church and state. But his exposition has earned broad
acceptance and has formed a backdrop from which many
of the more recent studies of church and state have secured
their over-all perspective.

Joachim Wach

Scholars who work within the broad context of the
sociology of religion have devised other typologies.
Joachim Wach, for example, including within his study
the religions of all mankind, concludes that three possible
relations exist between "religion and the state": (1) identity of state and cult, (2) the new faith, and (3) universal
religions.[3]

In the first category, society is characterized by a high
degree of homogeneity, in which the provinces of religion
and the state are commingled. Although many examples
of identity are found in the less advanced civilizations,
theocracy and Caesaro-papism also are characteristic of this
type.

The relationships in the second category are determined
by the fact that founded religions generally have a tendency to isolate themselves from the main community; they
rest upon expressions of secrecy and mystery. Examples of
this type are the Eleusinian and Dionysian mysteries within
Greece and the Shi'ite groups within Islam.

The third type is characterized by a "high degree of political development and an insistent claim for universality on the part of the religious community." The universalized aspects of Buddhism, Christianity, and Islam provide examples of this type.

Professor Wach also recognizes that transitional stages between the three types are historically evident. His view possesses the merit of being aware of the great significance of the founded religions; the complexities of the relations between church and state, beyond those embodied in the Western and Christian tradition; and the special character of the universal religions.

J. Milton Yinger

J. Milton Yinger analyzes the relations of church and state in the United States through the use of "three modes of relationship": (1) religious values as an important part of the value core of the societies, (2) religious values as instruments to win various kinds of political struggles, and (3) religious values as separate from the values of the state.[4] Yinger's classification appears to be somewhat limited by his tendency to view "religious values" almost solely from the standpoint of their socially integrative function. Church-state relations in the United States probably give evidence of more variations and functions than Yinger allows.

David O. Moberg

David O. Moberg also has provided a typology from the viewpoint of the sociology of religion and the American experience.[5] He states that there are five possible relationships between church and state and that they all have been observed in American history: (1) active hostility which results in the church's going underground has occurred only to small minority religions that have been persecuted as subversive; (2) each may intimately support the other, so that membership in one means membership in the other; (3) one church may be established by the state, with others tolerated; (4) the church may exist within a state because of the support it receives from another and stronger state, as in the case of foreign missions; or, as is the predominant pattern in United States history; (5) church and state may be legally separate, existing side by side, with distinct spheres of concern. These categories, although limited to the United States, show an awareness of the complexities of church-state relations.

Murray S. Stedman, Jr.

Murray S. Stedman, Jr., who has written a book "to advance an understanding of the relationships between religion and politics on both the empirical and the theoretical level," delineates seven types of situations that "arise often enough in the relationship between church and state so that they may be clearly identified": (1) where the church and the state leave each other alone, (2) where the government attempts to influence the church to gain government objectives, (3) where the church attempts to influence the government to gain church objectives, (4) where the church and the state cooperate to achieve mutually compatible ends, (5) where economic interests use the church's influence on government for the furtherance of economic objectives, (6) where the church defies the state, and (7) where one church fights another church over a government program.[6] Professor Stedman's typology is valuable in that it recognizes the variety of relationships that are possible, further extending the complexity.

Anson Phelps Stokes

Anson Phelps Stokes, as a consequence of a massive and detailed study of church-state relations, has created a fourfold typology: (1) imperial domination (subordination and often persecution of the church until A.D. 313), (2) church-state alliance (St. Augustine, in his *De Civitate Dei*), (3) ecclesiastical domination (Gregory the Great, A.D. 540-604), and (4) the ecclesiastical state or theocracy (the papal states and Calvin's Geneva). Stokes also develops four kinds of modern solutions that have been attempted to the age-old vexations of church and state relations: (1) the Erastian plan (the state determined the policy of the church and virtually controlled its conduct, as in czarist Russia), (2) the state-church plan (in which the official church is given much autonomy and other "sects" are allowed freedom, as in Great Britain), (3) the jurisdictional plan (equal status for several confessions, all supervised by the state, the pattern of the Peace of Westphalia), and (4) the separation plan (this may be benevolent, as in the United States, or hostile, as in Mexico in the first decades after the revolution).[7] Stokes's classification of church and state relations is richly suggestive and historically well-founded.

Thomas G. Sanders

More recently, Thomas G. Sanders, although confined to the Protestant tradition, has devised a typology which is largely based upon Protestant church and sect positions. He delineates five types of relationship: (1) God's regiments and man's vocation (Luther and Lutheranism), (2) Christian life without political compromise (the Anabaptists and Mennonites), (3) from theocracy to pacifism (the Quakers), (4) separationism (Baptists and others), and (5) moderation and pragmatism (Calvinism and Puritanism).[8] Sanders' typology has the advantage of being founded upon the historical views of churches themselves, rather than being restricted to intellectual abstractions, personalities, or events.

The foregoing review of some of the growing number of typologies that have been created in order to understand the historical and theoretical relations between church and state has been presented to illustrate the complexity of the subject and the current state of knowledge. At this time, no one typology appears to be universally acceptable, and each has one advantage or another. They seek to accomplish the task of scientific inquiry—to establish theoretical categories by which empirical data may be better understood—but in most instances they demonstrate that no one conception of the relations of church and state is presently normative.

In the remainder of this chapter and in the next chapter the typological relations of church and state will be discussed without the pretense that the problem of establishing an adequate typology has been settled. In fact, the primary purpose is not to explore the conditions for establishing a valid typology but, rather, to illustrate the several kinds of chief relationships that have existed historically between the church and the state. Each proposed type will not be exhaustively surveyed, but will be simply and superficially illustrated to give some understanding and appreciation of the relationships that are possible.[9] In this chapter two basic types of relationship will be discussed: (1) identity and (2) parallelism. In the following chapter four types of relationships will be explored: (1) paradoxism, (2) state dominance over the church, (3) church dominance over the state, and (4) transformationism.

IDENTITY

The relationship of identity is found wherever there are individuals and organizations who view the church and the state as having highly similar, if not identical, roles to play in society. The assumption is made that church and state should work together for the attainment of culturally agreed-upon aims. Troeltsch's "church" type lends itself to this formulation. The church seeks to be the universal agent within society whereby ethical and spiritual consensus is secured. The state becomes replete with religious symbols and meanings while the church looks upon itself as the sanctioned guide and support for at least the most ethicized activities of the state. It is inconceivable to the adherents of the relationship of identity that the individual could be a member of either church or state without being a member of the other.

Cultural Borrowing

The social and theoretical sources of the relationship of identity are manifold. First, the identity of church and state may rest upon the mutual borrowing of cultural elements. Hoult, for example, summarizes some of the ways in which the church historically borrowed from its cultural surroundings

. . . the virgin birth and messiah concepts, the doctrine of regeneration, baptism, communion, burial services, and the idea that the world is inhabited by the forces of evil pitted against those of good—common to Eastern and Near Eastern religions. Greek and Essene-like Jewish elements which were borrowed by Christianity were basic to the development of beliefs considered by laymen as uniquely Christian. Greek eschatology, dualism, asceticism, cosmology, anti-Judaism, and ideas on redemption and atoning sacrifice, all became part of Christianity. Much of this borrowing was facilitated by the work of Paul, who was strongly influenced by Gnosticism. Gnostic thought is credited with changing Christianity from a Jewish sect to a Christ-ism with universal aspirations, and with altering the gospel *of* Jesus to a gospel *about* him.[10]

Though Hoult's comments are restricted mainly to the formation of early Christianity, other examples of cultural borrowing, not always from the state, are available from every period of the history of Christianity.

Hoult's comments basically show religion's ability to borrow from culture, in this case from the surrounding religious culture. But religion also borrows from the non-religious aspects of culture. The theologian Langdon Gilkey points to this ability of religion in a discussion of the "sources of Protestant theology in America." He notes, as has previously been claimed, "the principle of the 'unity of American culture,' the manifest harmony between the secular and the religious elements in society, with the consequent interpenetration of each by the other—the secular influencing the religious and the religious the secular." [11] Gilkey also adds another "characteristic of American religion": "its almost total acceptance of the social, secular context of life." Gilkey continues:

American religiosity has traditionally viewed the state, the community, the market-place, the farm, and the family as fundamentally innocent, and even as revelatory and redemptive in character. The "world" has seldom been for the American a "fallen" place—a place of misery, sin, and frustration, a place from which either the wise, the good, or the religious man might legitimately seek to escape or flee. . . . Thus, American religion has never conceived of itself as being opposed to the world around it. In fact, much of what God was doing in history would, in the American view, be expected to appear in the social and political history of American life.[12]

Similarly, the state is in need of meanings, values, rituals, and other elements which are the hallmark of the church's functioning in society. The use of words and slogans on coins and in pledges, the employment of half-patriotic, half-religious ceremonies of all kinds illustrate the dependence of the state upon the church, the degree to which the state finds it necessary to clothe its interests with a religious garment. Lloyd Warner provides an illustration in this blending of state and of church interests in Memorial Day:

It is the thesis of this chapter that Memorial Day ceremonies and subsidiary rites (such as those of Armistice Day) of today, yesterday, and tomorrow are rituals of a sacred symbol system which functions periodically to unify the whole community, with its conflicting symbols and its opposing, autonomous churches and associations. It is contended here that in the Memorial Day ceremony the anxieties which man has about death are confronted with a system of sacred beliefs about death which gives the individuals involved and the collectivity of individuals a feeling of well-being. . . . Memorial Day is a cult of the dead which organizes and integrates various faiths and national and class groups into a sacred unity. It is a cult of the dead organized around the community cemeteries.[13]

Natural Law

Second, the relationship of identity also draws upon natural law. The theory of natural law assumes that there are principles available for the guidance of individual and collective behavior that are derived from universal awareness, prior to specifically revealed contributions. These are derived from the order of nature in which man exists. Thus, historically the state has been able to appeal to standards for the governing of its citizens that extend beyond the special claims of particular religious groups. It is on the assumption of the natural law that the state is able to appeal to an effective moral consensus, especially in times of crisis.

But historically the church also has made its appeals to the natural law as being a creation of God and, therefore, necessarily binding not only upon the body of believers but upon all citizens. The higher demands of religion may be derived from revelation, but the churchly demands for an ordered social existence commonly are argued on the basis of principles derived from the natural law. To the extent to which appeals are made by the church and the state to the natural law, there is a basis for the relationship of identity.

Providence

Third, the generalized concept of Providence also is a source of the relationship of identity. Both church and state frequently acknowledge the common rule of Providence in and between their affairs. American colonial history, for example, provides many examples in which the colonist saw the hand of Providence guiding the affairs of both church and state. At times the emphasis upon Providence tended to obscure even the separateness of the social institutions of church and state.

Such a view of the identity of church and state within the idea of Providence is reminiscent of the identity of religious communion and civil community in the early history of Israel. W. Robertson Smith has commented upon the identity of church and state in that time:

When David in the bitterness of his heart complains of those who "have driven him out from connection with the heritage of Jehovah," he represents them as saying to him, "Go, serve other Gods." In driving him to seek refuge in another land and another nationality, they compel him to change his religion, for a man's religion is part of his political connection. "Thy sister," says Naomi to Ruth, "is gone back unto her people and unto her Gods"; and Ruth replies, "Thy people shall be my people, and thy God my God": the change of nationality involves a change of cult.[14]

From such sources, then, the idea of the identity of church and state is nourished.

Constantine

Relationships of identity between church and state have been maintained in many periods of Western civilization. In this connection the role of Constantine in creating what may be called "the imperial state church" comes readily to mind.[15] Constantine saw that if the Roman Empire had one emperor, one law, and one citizenship for all free men, it ought to have one religion to complete the process of unification. In an effort to achieve this added element of unity, a law was passed in A.D. 319 by which the clergy were exempted from the public obligations that were the lot of the wealthy of the empire. The right to receive legacies was granted in A.D. 321; by this right the corporate privileges of the church were acknowledged. In the same year, work on Sunday was forbidden to the people of the cities. In this period, too, private heathen sacrifices were prohibited, gifts were made to the clergy, and great churches were erected in Rome, Jerusalem, Bethlehem, and elsewhere under Constantine's auspices.

Also, in an effort to create a basis for political and military unity as well as to create a single church in both the East and the West, Constantine moved his capital to the rebuilt Byzantium which later was called by his own name. The achievement of a state church represented the identity of church and state in the Constantinian period.

Crusades

The Crusades of the later Middle Ages are another example of the way in which historically the functions of church and state have been blended into a unity. From the standpoint of their purpose the Crusades can be viewed as failures, since they made no permanent conquest of the Holy Land; they failed to retard the advance of Islam; and their cost in lives and treasure was inestimable. Yet they represent a significant example of the amalgam of a high spirit of religious devotion with military and commercial interests that were given effect by a number of political leaders and states.

In one part of the Crusades, for example, Alexius I (1081-1118), who was a stronger ruler than his immediate predecessors in Constantinople, appealed to Pope Urban II for aid. Urban responded favorably to Alexius' messengers in March, 1095, and proclaimed in the synod held at Clermont (eastern France) in the following November that the enterprise of relieving the hard-pressed Alexius was in reality the general rescue of the holy places from Muslim control. Although Urban issued the call, it was the armies raised from the cities of Europe that, under feudal lords interspersed with religious and other personalities, waged the actual battles of the Crusades. These and other aspects of the Crusades indicate the manner in which church and state were conjoined in mutual and identical purposes.

United States

The relationship of identity between church and state has not been absent in the United States from the beginning of its history until now.[16] Many Christians today almost eagerly identify Americanism and Christianity. They aver that Christianity has formed the basis for American democracy and that American democracy in turn has nourished a particularly pure form of Christianity. One of the most widely acclaimed and criticized statements of this American identity of church and state appeared during wartime in *Fortune*. According to *Fortune*'s editorial:

As the leading democracy of the world, therefore, the United States is perforce the leading practical exponent of Christianity. The United States is not Christian in any formal religious sense: its churches are not full on Sundays and its citizens transgress the precepts freely. But it is Christian in the sense of absorption. The basic teachings of Christianity are in its blood stream. . . . Christian idealism is manifest in the culture and habits of the people, in the arguments that orators and politicians use to gain their ends; in the popular ideas of good taste, which control advertising, movies, radio, and all forms of public opinion; in the laws, the manners, and the standards of our people.[17]

In the years following the Second World War, moreover, a number of perceptive writers have critically examined the relationship of identity between church and state. A. Roy Eckhardt has shown that the mid-twentieth-century "religious revival" is highly tinged with secular as well as sentimental notions of the nature of the Christian faith.[18] Martin E. Marty declares that a new shape is desired for American religion, since contemporary religion has become "religion-in-general."[19] Will Herberg has advanced the thesis that the "American way of life" forms the basically unitive value system on which Protestants, Roman Catholics, and Jews, as well as others, are integrated. He thinks that there is today a "faith in faith" by which the precise nature of religious commitment is less important than that one have a sense of commitment to the American way of life.[20]

In modern times the identity of church and state has been asserted by some advocates of religion. European Catholic political parties have regularly tended to identify the Christian faith with existing stable and conservative governments. Some Roman Catholics in the United States have been prone to identify traditional Americanism with traditional Catholicism. Similarly, Protestant fundamentalist groups have tended to take the part of what they consider to be true Americanism. At times they are opposed to a strong federal government, public schools, labor unions, progressive income taxes, the United

Nations, and other features of present-day America. Indeed, these fundamentalist groups tend to look upon other
Protestants, who support social innovation, as being
"reds" or traitors. The American Council of Churches
epitomizes this position and regularly castigates the National Council of the Churches of Christ in the United
States of America for its allegedly leftist leanings. No wonder, then, that Ralph Roy terms these fundamentalist
groups "apostles of discord." [21]

PARALLELISM

Yet all of these views may do an injustice to the complexity of society. At every time, even when state churches
have existed, there have been dissident groups of religious
people who have been skeptical of the claims of those who
advocated the identity of church and state. During Constantine's time there were sectarian Christian groups
which stood outside the emperor's acceptance and identification with Christianity. So, too, in nations where there
is a state church, such as modern Great Britain, there also
may be a toleration of sectarian religious organizations
which in themselves stand opposed to the identification
of church and state. Similarly, in current America the
culture religion described by recent analysts fails to do
full justice to such factors as the rise of neo-orthodoxy as
a theological movement in Protestantism, the persistence
of essentially Baptist views of the separation of church and
state, and the constant origination of holiness sects among
the lower classes.

Reinhold Niebuhr has remarked that "traditional and
institutional religions . . . tend to impart the aura of the

absolute to the existing order of things. . . . Yet religion is never exhausted in these corruptions." [22] The ability of religion to transcend the temporal also is well known in the history of Western civilization. In fact, at certain points in history the two social institutions of church and state are quite separate and even opposed. This stance or reality constitutes parallelism.

Parallelism is born in the tension that exists almost everywhere between what is and what ought to be. Even though the church in a given historical period may be broadly identified with the total culture of a nation, elements within it may keep it from being completely identified with the national culture. The people of the church may think of themselves as being somehow and somewhat different from the general body of the citizenry which accepts the operative requirements of the state. The assumption may be made that in the over-all design of things the church and the state by some mystical transaction operate harmoniously together, although on specific points of interrelationship they may not be identical or even mutually responsive. The doctrine of creation (the essential goodness of all things) is coupled with the doctrine of evil (the fallen nature of man) in parallelism, and the result is interpreted in terms of two spheres of more or less paralleling responsibility.

Augustine

Daniel Bell describes the essentially Augustinian or parallelistic conception of man and society as a reaction to the fear of the masses who played a destructive role in the Roman Republic. He says:

Early Christian theory justifies its fear of the masses with a theory about human nature. In the religious terms of Augustine—as, later, in the secularized version of Hobbes—the Earthly City bore an ineradicable stain of blood: in Paradise there was neither private property nor government; property and police were the consequence of the Fall of Man; property and police were signs, therefore, not of Man's civilization but of his corruption; they were necessary means of keeping Man in check.[23]

But whatever the language employed and no matter whether the situation is ancient or modern, there are those who cannot accept the identity of church and state.

Historically, Augustine's great treatise *The City of God,* begun in the dark days following the capture of Rome by Alaric and finished about A.D. 426, constitutes not only a philosophy of history but a powerful and persistent theory of the parallel relations between church and state. Augustine believed that the worship of the old gods had given Rome neither strength nor civic virtue. That Roman religion failed was considered a blessing by Augustine, not a true loss. As he describes history, Augustine notes that "two cities have been formed by two loves: the earthly by love of self, even to the contempt of God; the heavenly by the love of God, even to the contempt of self." [24] These two loves and their respective cities are symbolized in the persons of Cain and Abel. The earthly city has as its leading representatives heathen Babylon and Rome. The city of God is composed of all those persons who confess themselves to be strangers and pilgrims on the earth.

The earthly city is not all bad; it operates on the basis of peace and civil order. Having love of self as its primary principle, it recognizes the need to repress disorder and to create a measure of security and justice for each person. But the earthly city must pass away in order that the city of God may grow.

Those who compose the city of God are the elect who are now in the visible church, although not all in that church are truly elect. Said Augustine: "Therefore the church even now is the kingdom of Christ, and the kingdom of Heaven. Accordingly, even now His saints reign with Him, though otherwise than as they shall reign hereafter; and yet though the tares grow in the Church along with the wheat, they do not reign with Him." [25]

So, in Augustine's view, there are essentially two social institutions, the church and the state. These are divinely ordered even though they differ greatly in their composition and purpose. Augustine's views not only contributed heavily to forming the philosophic basis for the theory of the medieval papacy; they also have outcropped in many of those churches and sects which adhere to some degree of separation of church and state.

Dante and Others

Augustine's views were reinterpreted in the medieval period by several noted thinkers. One of these was the great Italian poet Dante Alighieri (1265-1321), whose Latin treatise *On Monarchy* was composed in the early part of the fourteenth century. In this work Dante holds that peace is the best condition of mankind and that it is most effectively maintained by an emperor. Thus, the power of empire rightfully belongs to Rome. But, according to Dante, it is necessary that there be another agency in society to assist man to his temporal happiness. The papacy is that agency. Dante taught that both the church and the state are derived directly from God and that neither should interfere with the other. Dante, in his even-handed way, was not only resisting the prior papal interpretations of church supremacy, but was laying the groundwork for the doctrine of parallelism in the relationships of church and state.

In the same period there were others who supported an essentially parallel relationship between church and state. John of Paris (1265?-1306) taught that both church and state were dependent for their parallel sovereignties upon the people and that neither has a right to interfere with the other. Marsilius of Padua (?-1342?), a rector of the University of Paris and a learned man in medicine, wrote the *Defensor Pacis* in 1324, claiming that the basis of all power rests in the people. The power of the state rests upon the whole body of citizens and the power of the church upon the whole body of Christian believers. The leaders both of church and of state are appointed by the legislative power inherent within the people and these executive officers are responsible to the people. The views of Marsilius and others strengthened the idea that there is a clear separation between church and state and that the people play an important part in the maintenance and leadership of both institutions.

Parallelism as an interpretation of the relations of church and state became especially pointed during the sixteenth century when the Anabaptists, the Mennonites and others of the left-wing Protestant tradition severely criticized any attachment by the church to the state. To them, the church was good and the state was bad. Thus, the fourth article of the Schleitheim Confession of Faith (1527) clearly declares the Anabaptist basis for the separation of believers from unbelievers in all spheres of life:

We are agreed on separation: A separation shall be made from the evil and from the wickedness which the devil planted in the world; in this manner, simply that we shall not have fellowship with them [the wicked] and not run with them in the multitude of their abominations. This is the way it is: Since all who do not walk in the obedience of faith, and have not united themselves with God so that they wish to do His will, are a great abomination before God, it is not possible for anything to grow or issue from them except abominable things. For truly all creatures are in but two classes, good and bad, believing and unbelieving, darkness and light, the world and those who [have come] out of the world, God's temple and idols, Christ and Belial; and none can have part with the other. . . . He further admonishes us to withdraw from Babylon and the earthly Egypt that we may not be partakers of the pain and suffering which the Lord will bring upon them.[26]

The Anabaptist doctrine of church and state was not based upon a clearly articulated and rational description of the relations of the two social institutions. The Anabaptist thought of the church as a separated group in society, quite different from the state churches of the time, a body characterized by repentance, justification, and regeneration. Authentic baptism in the view of the Anabaptists was the sign of the new condition. The state, on the other hand, was bad in the same sense that all of the unredeemed sectors of the general society were bad. Only two kingdoms existed—that of God, of which the Anabaptists were members, and that of the devil, in which all other persons and social institutions are citizens. Thus, the Anabaptists did not develop a substantial doctrine of separation of church and state; rather, they advocated the separation of the two bodies of believers from the rest of an evil society. Holding to this view, they naturally be-

lieved that the true Christian should not hold political
office. The state was a necessary evil, and the magistrate
was to be prayed for, but most of the Anabaptists held
that the Christian had more important things to do than
serve in state offices.

Even to this day and in the United States, those communions which follow in the left-wing Protestant tradition continue to distinguish sharply between the two
spheres of society.[27] One such denomination is the Mennonite, which bases its Christian practice upon the teachings of Menno Simons (1492-1559). Guy F. Hershberger
affirms the Mennonite doctrine of the separation of church
and state:

At this point it is sufficient to say that there never has been
anything like a truly Christian state on a national scale, even
though there have been national states which have professed
Christianity. . . . But as long as the entire society is not
Christian, the state will need to employ the coercive means
which it always has used. It will continue to be primarily an
organization for the maintenance of law and order, by coercive means, in a sinful society. A truly Christian society would
be something quite different from anything which we know
today. . . .[28]

Through these and other historical persons, events, and
teachings, it is clear that parallelism, involving some degree of separation of the social institutions of church and
state, is factually grounded.

The separatist position in the United States has its
organized expression in the organization called Protestants
and Other Americans United for Separation of Church
and State. This educational and nonprofit corporation was
organized in 1947, with headquarters in the nation's capi-

tal and with regional offices in New York, Chicago, and Los Angeles. In a manifesto, issued on November 20, 1947, the purpose of the organization was stated as follows: "Its single and only purpose is to assure the maintenance of the American principle of separation of church and state upon which the Federal Constitution guarantees liberty to all the people and all churches of this Republic." The organization also publishes a monthly, sixteen-page journal with a printing of 175,000, entitled *Church and State: A Monthly Review*. But the organization is more than a study group; it sends representatives into the courts and before legislative committees to plead its case for what it considers to be the traditional American doctrine of extreme separation of church and state.

The fact that church and state have been viewed as separate or parallel in their functions does not necessarily lead to the conclusion that hostile relations always exist between them. There are many persons, of course, who have asserted that church and state stand in some degree of hostility toward each other, but there are others who think that the relationship can be benevolent—as is illustrated in the relationship between Gregory III and Pepin the Short. Again, church and state may be viewed as separate entities related to each other through codes or contracts—as is illustrated in the relationships between Victor Emmanuel and Pius IX in the Vatican Contract or in the Peace of Westphalia. In all of these relationships, however, aside from their distinctive historical content and spirit, there is upheld a parallel view of the relations between church and state.

6

Church-State in Western History (continued)

Two fundamental types of relations between church and state have been discussed briefly in the previous chapter: identity and parallelism. Four additional types will be outlined in this chapter: (1) paradoxism, (2) state dominance over the church, (3) church dominance over the state, and (4) transformationism.

To some degree, these four are simply variations of identity and parallelism. Each assumes a degree of mutuality and of separation, however, which makes it difficult to classify them as belonging to either category. Yet it must be borne in mind throughout the discussion of these two chapters that the six forms in themselves are largely ideational constructs which are not intended to be logically exclusive categories, but guideposts to an understanding of the variety and the complexity, both past and present, of church and state relations.[1] Also, the illustrations are not offered as proof, but merely as examples, chosen usually from a wide field, of the kinds of historical occurrences which give clarity to the typology. Even the illustrations at times may be considered as applying to more than one category.[2]

PARADOXISM

A third type of relationship sees the church and the state in paradox. In a sense, this type of relationship is deeply appreciative of both identity and parallelism. It sees that the required coherence within society appears to be impossible if church and state, those two powerful social institutions with deep influence over the lives of individuals, are deemed to be so distinctive and lacking in interaction as to create, in Augustine's terms, two cities, each of which is strikingly different from the other. A view other than identity raises other problems. Is there not one creation, and are not both the church and the state the creation of one Providence? How can it be that the one holy and consistent Providence would create two social orders that are not harmoniously related to each other?

On the other hand, the position of identity leads almost inescapably to certain perplexities. The assumption is made that there are two social institutions, church and state, that possess a high degree of mutuality in their founding, nature, and goals. But their language, organization, and other features are often dissimilar. Also, historical evidence shows that identity has not been the universal relationship of church and state and that at many points in Western civilization church and state have either run on parallel courses or have established some other sort of relationship.

Paradoxism is the attempt to have the best of the two worlds of identity and parallelism. Yet it is more than an intellectual ploy, a device invented to solve a knotty problem. It is a position that has been held by sincere intellectuals throughout the course of Western civilization. Paradoxism also has taken concrete sociological form and, thus, is no mere intellectual construct, but a social reality.

Those individuals and organizations which support the relationship of identity are essentially conservative. They look upon both church and state as social instrumentalities that have a stake in each other to such an extent that each must minimize any separatist tendencies in order to protect harmony and mutuality. The individuals and organizations that support parallelism are mainly left-wing liberal or radical. They see the essential form of each social institution as being perverted when identity is sought and maintained. They believe in the separation of the social orders in society.

Paradoxism is commonly maintained by the centerists, the middle group in society. They approach the relations of church and state with a "both-and," rather than an "either-or." Their task admittedly is more difficult, since they regularly are in the position of being compromisers or adjusters of the two social institutions to each other. They do not approach the relations of church and state as "dualists," as H. Richard Niebuhr asserts.[3] If they were "dualists," they would more properly fit into the category of parallelism. They are "dualists" only in the sense that they recognize the separateness of church and state. In actuality, they hold to a paradoxical position, for they believe that the two social institutions, while separate, interact in ways that seem at times to be logically inconsistent.

A case in point occurred in November, 1966, when the

United States Supreme Court refused to review a decision of the Maryland Court of Appeals that voided state aid to three church-related colleges and approved it for a fourth. The top court of Maryland, in passing its judgment, invoked the Supreme Court's own test when it banned compulsory Bible reading in the public schools in 1963: "To withstand the strictures of the Establishment clause there must be a secular legislative purpose and a primary effect that neither advances nor inhibits religion." It did not matter that the grants were specifically limited to non-religious purposes—construction of dormitories and science buildings. Instead, the court asked whether each church college was so permeated by religion that a secular grant would automatically aid its sectarian ambiance. How to measure such religiosity? The court provided six criteria, ranging from the degree of church control and the number of compulsory religious courses to the "image of the college in the community." However inviting to subjective judgment, the test clearly barred grants to two Catholic colleges, one of which planned to put crucifixes in each new, tax-paid science classroom. Western Maryland's Methodism was more elusive, but clear church control barred that grant, too. Only Hood (United Church of Christ) passed the test, because, among other open-minded policies, it welcomes teachers and students of all faiths and of none. Although the Maryland decision applies only to that state, it illustrates the complexities and the ambiguities of church-state relations from the standpoint of paradoxism.

Martin Luther

Although the doctrine of paradoxism can be seen clearly in Paul and Marcion, its classical expression was formu-

lated by Martin Luther. Luther held an intensely theocratic view of man and society. Luther was not a modern-
day sociologist in his viewing of the social orders in society,
but a Christian theologian who sought to view everything
in life from the starting point of God. Thus, the overarching construct in Luther's mind was the divine sovereignty
over the whole of life. All aspects of life, including the
state, therefore, were to be accounted for on the basis of
their relation to God.

Luther also was deeply impressed with the fact that
man as a sinner possesses incalculable ability to pervert
the will of God in his social life as well as in his individual
existence. On the basis of such a view, Luther found the
Roman Catholic Church of his time wanting. He found it
difficult to rationalize his intensely pure and righteous
conception of the holy God with the institutional claims
and practices of that church. Luther called for a "reformation" of the Roman Catholic Church on the basis of theological principles derived from the Bible. God's sovereignty as expressed in the Bible appeared to him to be
strikingly different from those "authorities" exemplified
by the Roman Church. The Reformation represents on the
churchly side Luther's efforts to refashion the church as
a social institution in consonance with God's sovereignty
as revealed in the Bible.

On the side of society, however, Luther's views on the
state led him to the position of paradoxism. Luther easily
recognized that there is no simple identity between the
church and the state. He was impressed with the fact that
Jesus spoke about the things of Caesar and the realm of
God, a kingdom of this world and a heavenly kingdom.
Those who sought to live by the Sermon on the Mount
were part of God's kingdom of salvation, while those who

did not were still part of his wider kingdom of creation and sovereignty.

On the basis of such distinctions, Luther divided all men into two classes:

. . . the first belonged to the kingdom of God, the second to the kingdom of the world. Those belonging to the kingdom of God are all true believers in Christ and are subject to Christ. For Christ is the King and Lord in the kingdom of God. . . . Now observe, these people need no secular sword or law. And if all the world were composed of real Christians, that is, true believers, no prince, king, sword, or law would be needed. All who are not Christians belong to the kingdom of the world and are under the law. Since few believe and still fewer live a Christian life, do not resist the evil, and themselves do no evil, God has provided for non-Christians a different government outside the Christian estate and God's kingdom, and has subjected them to the sword, so that, even though they would do so, they cannot practice their wickedness, and that, if they do, they may not do it without fear nor in peace and prosperity.[4]

These two institutions, or "regiments," as Luther called them, are intrinsically different, but not essentially opposed to each other, since both are created by God. Luther did not demean the state, but saw God's design and purpose in its existence and leaders. Regarding "worldly government" and "temporal blessings," Luther was able to say of God:

For He gives to rulers so much property, honor, and power, to be possessed by them above others, in order that they may serve Him by administering this righteousness. Thus God himself is the founder, lord, master, protector, and rewarder of both kinds of righteousness. There is no human ordinance or authority in either, but each is altogether a divine thing.[5]

Thus, Luther thought of church and state as the creations of God which require the loyal submission of the believer to both. The state is the worldly regiment and the left hand of the kingdom; the church is God's right hand and his spiritual regiment. The two institutions do not represent a higher and a lower order; rather, as divine creations they both are approved by God and possess an intricate relationship to each other.

The paradoxical character of Luther's views of church and state are readily seen in his answer to the question whether governmental officials can be good Christians. He answers this question affirmatively. In support of this view, he claims, first, that the state is a divinely established institution and, therefore, the proper service of the state is service rendered to God. Second, he claims that the good Christian is one who fulfills his "vocation" with a concern for others rather than for himself. When the Christian political official acts out of such a concern, he is performing a work of love.

The paradoxical position of Luther is also shown in his teaching that the Christian may properly be a critic of the state and even engage in civil disobedience. The state is to be obeyed, says Luther, when it operates on proper principles within its own allotted sphere. The princes properly are to be protected against peasant-inspired revolutions. But when the rulers are tempted by pride and fail to be subject to God's Word, they are to be rebuked and resisted. Luther makes this latter point in connection with his exposition of Psalm 82:

So, then, this first verse teaches that to rebuke rulers is not seditious, provided it is done in the way here described; namely, by the office to which God has committed that duty, and through God's Word, spoken publicly, boldly, and honestly. To rebuke rulers in this way is, on the contrary, a praiseworthy, noble, and rare virtue, and would be far more seditious, if a preacher were not to rebuke the sins of the rulers, for then he makes people angry and sullen, and strengthens the wickedness of the tyrants and becomes a partaker in it, and bears responsibility for it. Thus God might be angered and might allow rebellion to come as a penalty.[6]

While Luther probably developed the doctrine of paradoxism to a greater degree than any other person, he was not alone in holding this position. Examples of it can be found in many times and places, including our own. Present-day Lutheranism in the United States, for example, is highly influenced by Luther's paradoxical views and, indeed, paradoxism has been a lively and accepted option by many non-Lutherans.

Present-day Lutherans have expressed the doctrine of paradoxism in modern and studied form. For example, the Commission on Church and State Relations in a Pluralistic Society, sponsored by the Board of Social Ministry of the Lutheran Church in America, began its work in 1961 and in 1963 issued a comprehensive statement which explicated the traditional Lutheran perspective on church-state relations.[7] Similarly, the Lutheran Church-Missouri Synod was the first Protestant denomination in this country to authorize a major study of church-state relations. Authorized in 1956 by the Board of Directors of the Lutheran Church-Missouri Synod, the study, published in 1964, gives extensive support to the paradoxical position of Luther.[8]

STATE DOMINANCE

Another view of the relations of church and state holds that the state is dominant over the church. In this type of

relationship, the separateness of the two social institutions
is readily admitted. Both church and state exist for opera-
tionally different purposes. The state exists in order to
regularize and protect the universal interests and needs of
men. The church exists as a voluntary organization devoted to the achievement of high ends.

The state, however, is necessary for the establishment
and maintenance of the social order. Society cannot get
along without the state. The state exists even where several churches are permitted and even protected. The
church fulfills its functions only within the broader context of the social reality which the state, as the apex of all
of the social institutions, provides. Where there is tension
and even conflict between the two social institutions, it is
assumed that the church must be subordinate to the state.
Only by such a position on the part of the church can the
general social order be preserved.

Insofar as the church implements the social harmony
required by the state, it is a "free institution." Where its
teachings and practices are disharmonious or opposed to
those of the state, the church must give way. This view of
the relations of church and state obviously is held more
often by those who are impressed with the basic requirements of the state than it is by those who hold to the
primacy of the church as a social regulator and force.

The dominance of the state over the church currently
is seen in the United States in those restrictions and limitations imposed by state regulations upon the incorporation,
property ownership, safety, and zoning of the church.[9]
Similarly, religious liberty in the United States does not
permit those religious practices which tend to injure
health, safety, or the morals of even those who accept such
views. Flagellation, snake-handling, and polygamy, for

example, are prohibited by law as practices inimical to the public welfare.

Yet this distinction is not always clearly made. For example, the Supreme Court of California ruled in 1964 that the use of peyote, a hallucinatory drug, in religious ceremonies does not violate the state narcotics laws. Indian tribes, the court noted in passing judgment upon two accused members of the Native American Church, which is incorporated under California law, are known to practice the religion of peyotism in Arizona, Montana, Oklahoma, Saskatchewan, and Wisconsin as well as California. "To forbid the use of peyote is to remove the theological heart of peyotism," the court said.[10]

The court, in effect, found that peyote rituals are not so socially harmful as to overrule the claim of religious freedom made by the Native American Church. Apparently, the dominant consideration in allowing the exemption was the court's respect for cultural pluralism. Thus, in part, the court concluded:

In a mass society, which presses at every point toward conformity, the protection of a self-expression, however unique, of the individual and the group becomes ever more important. The varying currents of the sub-cultures that flow into the mainstream of our national life give it depth and beauty. We preserve a greater value than an ancient tradition when we protect the rights of the Indians who honestly practiced an old religion in using peyote one night at a meeting in a desert hogan near Needles, California.[11]

Justin

The dominance of the state over the church is less a theological principle than a political reality in the long course of Western civilization. The lives of the apologists in the second century, for example, are understood mainly on the basis that the Roman government was hostile toward the early Christians, accusing them of atheism and anarchy. Justin, called the Martyr, among others, sought to show that Christianity was not what the Roman rulers thought it was. In his *Apology* he claimed that if Christians were to be condemned at all, they should be punished for definite, proved crimes and not merely for being Christians. He asserted that Christians were atheists only in the sense that they believed that the popular gods of Rome were demons unworthy of worship, and that in fact the Christians held the true God in high esteem. He averred that Christians did not seek to reduce the Roman state to anarchy, but simply wished to be obedient to their higher calling by God in Jesus the Christ. Justin's efforts, then, reflect the fact that the church in his time was dominated by the state.

Nestorius

The manner in which the state has been employed to settle theological disputes and to regulate the life of the church is illustrated in the life of Nestorius, Patriarch of Constantinople in the fifth century, an able theologian who would not admit that there were two persons in Christ. He strongly emphasized the reality and completeness of the human in the Christ. As a consequence, he was bitterly opposed by Cyril, Patriarch of Alexandria (412-444).

Cyril not only engaged in theological controversy with Nestorius, but also appealed to Emperor Theodosius II, to Empress Eudocia, and to the emperor's sister, Pulcheria, claiming that Nestorius' doctrines destroyed all basis for salvation. Cyril also presented his case to Pope Celestine I (422-432), who ordered Nestorius to recant or be excommunicated. As a means of solving the theological debate, the two emperors, Theodosius II of the East and Valentinian III of the West, called a general council to meet in Ephesus in 431. Although the council ended in a victory for Cyril, the theological dispute continued, with political factors being as important in the debate as the theological. Nestorius finally was banished to Upper Egypt.

John Wyclif

Although the view of the dominance of the state over the church has been held mainly by those who have been impressed with the requirements of the state, it has been advocated at times by deeply religious persons. John Wyclif (?-1384) held such a view. Wyclif was strongly opposed to the wealth of the church of his time and was highly critical of clerical interference, especially that of the popes, in the political life of England. In 1376, in lectures given at Oxford University, he presented his views, holding, like Luther, that God is the supreme sovereign over the whole of life. God gives both religious and political offices as fiefs (in the feudal fashion), which are permitted on condition of faithful service. If the user abuses God's trust, he forfeits his tenure. Wyclif taught that a bad ecclesiastical leader loses his claim to his office and that his temporal possessions may be taken from him by the civil ruler, to whom God has given the lordship of temporal things, as he has of spiritual things to the church.

Wyclif was called to answer for his views before the Bishop of London, William Courtenay, and in the same

year, 1377, Pope Gregory XI issued five bulls that ordered
Wyclif's arrest and examination. However, Wyclif was so
protected by his friends at court and by the populace that
these proceedings were not carried out.

Erastianism

"Erastianism" is a term which describes a number of
situations in which Protestant churches in Europe and
England were subservient to the state. The originator of
the principle was presumedly Hugo Grotius (1583-1645),
the jurist, historian, and founder of international law. The
immediate social context for Grotius' views was the
Netherlands of his time, in which a "state's rights" and a
national party were in conflict. Theologically, the dispute
centered on a disagreement between Arminianism and
Calvinism, in which Calvinism turned out to be the victor.
One of the consequences, however, was the development
of the view that the church (including the established
church and sects) secured its standing and privileges by
reason of the prior authority of the government.

Henry VIII (1491-1547), King of England from 1509 to
1547, epitomizes the Erastian doctrine. Admittedly, a host
of factors were involved in the English Reformation.
Henry was infatuated with Anne Boleyn. He wished to
invalidate his marriage to Catherine of Aragon both because of her seeming inability to bear more children and
because of her strong loyalty to Spain. The heady stream
of Reformation ideas was current in England. Henry, in
addition, was in danger of losing his authority over the
nobility. He also had tremendous egotism, which led him
to favor a personal despotism in which he, as king, claimed
supremacy for the state over all elements in English so-

ciety. The net result was the establishment of the church as a body under the full and final control of the state. It is of interest to note that throughout his life Henry remained orthodox in his doctrinal views.

Elizabeth I (1533-1603), Queen of England from 1558 to 1603, was the daughter of Henry VIII and Anne Boleyn. She inherited the Tudor concept of strong rule, which she related to various features of English society. Soon after becoming queen (1559), she re-established Protestantism through the Acts of Supremacy and Uniformity. In 1585 a law was enacted which declared it treason for a Catholic priest to set foot in England. These actions, supported by Elizabeth, may in part be interpreted as expressing her favoritism for the established Church of England, but in reality they express the Erastian principle, by which it was the state that determined the official religious life of the national citizenry.

Erastianism also has been practiced in other times and places. Especially demonic forms were found in Adolf Hitler's National Socialism, under which education, law, religion, and other features of German life were forcibly made subservient to the state. The Soviet Union, especially under the leadership of Joseph Stalin, provides another illustration of the supremacy of the state over the church.

Mysticism

The dominance of the state over the church has found expression far beyond the instances noted. Often, where it exists, it seems to be nourished not only by strong theories and practices on the part of those who control the state, but also by attitudes of withdrawal, asceticism, mysticism, monasticism, and other forms of withdrawal into religion and away from the state and the social order. Mysticism, for example, brought Eckhart (1260-1327), a German Dominican, not only to the point of regarding society's social institutions as highly irrelevant to the religious life, but also to the conclusion that even churchly observances are of little value, since the springs of the mystical experience are found in direct union with God. Thomas à Kempis (1380?-1471), a pupil of the Brethren of the Common Life and the author of the famed *Imitation of Christ*, spent most of his long life in the monastery of Mount St. Agnes, far from the complexities either of ecclesiastical or of political concerns. Even Montanism, a movement within the general church of the second century, by reason of its ascetic practices, drew many Christians away not only from a responsibility for the state, but also from the growing worldliness of the church.

Mysticism does not in itself clearly assert the supremacy of the state over the church, but it assumes the unworthiness and even the unreality of all historical experience. It sharply differentiates between the existential realms of particularity and limitation and the essential realm of transcendental essence in which God alone is real. Mysticism, therefore, in the words of Reinhold Niebuhr, "flees from the tensions and incomplete harmonies of history to an undifferentiated unity of life in eternity." [12] Thus, mysticism provides a social vacuum in which various powers, such as the state, find their ready and unresisted fulfillment. Mysticism does not encourage state supremacy over the church, but permits it by default.

American Negro Religion

In the United States a prime example of withdrawal from society on the part of religious people is illustrated in American Negro religion. The escapist and emotional forms which some of this religion has taken has defined by default the acceptance of the dominance of the state over the church. The combination of piety and withdrawal from political affairs is noted by Willard L. Sperry: "Way back in the 1830's Harriet Martineau noted the advertisements in the New Orleans papers of the sales of occasional lots of 'pious negroes' as being an especially good bargain. They would give no trouble here and now. The modern radical Negro agitator regards his pious brothers as one of his liabilities; they are an obstacle to the full and final freedom of the race." [13] Although American Negro religion has taken several forms, and they all are not of one type, it may be fair to say that in the main this religious expression has accepted the dominance of the state over the church.

Some parts of American Negro religion currently stand out in stark contrast with that previously described. The social picture, however, is mixed. Undoubtedly the activities favoring civil rights for Negroes owe much of their rationale and power to the religious faith of the Negro churches and their leaders. The church connections of such leaders as Martin Luther King, Jr., Ralph Abernathy, Hosea Williams, Andrew Young, and Milton Galamison are apparent. In general, these and other church-inspired and church-connected Negro leaders do not take refuge in other-worldly complacency so far as human rights are concerned. They have given new meaning to American Negro religion.

On the other hand, two qualifications need to be made regarding the total civil rights movement. First, many of the Negro leaders themselves are not related organizationally to the American Negro churches, but find their rationale for human rights in secular historical sources. Second, a number of Negro churches and their leaders, especially in the South, are divided on strategic issues. William G. McLoughlin, for example, claims that "Negro churchgoers are badly split" and provides the following example:

Dr. Joseph H. Jackson, president of the National Baptist Convention, U.S.A., Inc., the largest Negro denomination in the United States with 5,500,000 members, so consistently pulled back from civil rights activities and deplored sit-ins and demonstrations on their behalf that Martin Luther King, Jr., felt obliged to lead a schism from this group in 1962. Only a minority followed him.[14]

It is clear that American Negro religion is no longer complacently oriented toward piety but is a growing force combining its energies and outlook with other elements in American society to utilize the state for the achievement of human-rights goals.

Certainly Negro religion in the United States is historically complex. Joseph R. Washington, Jr., believes that it has changed over the years, but that it is and always has been indifferent to the great Christian mission, lacking in formal theology, given to emotional escapism, and founded more in the frustrated desire for freedom than in a truly religious spirit.[15]

These and other historical expressions indicate that the relationship of state dominance over the church has been significant and widespread.

CHURCH DOMINANCE

The dominance of the state by the church, which constitutes another basic relationship, is more consonant with parallelism and paradoxism than it is with identity. It accepts the two social institutions of church and state, yet it is unable to accept the view that the two social institutions are operating on parallel courses, perhaps brought together within the idea of Providence. Nor is it able to accept, with paradoxism, the view that the transcendent God utilizes both church and state, perhaps in equal but different measure, to work his will in human history. Those individuals and organizations which advocate church dominance over the state clearly hold that the two institutions are not completely conjoined in mutual purposes, and they cannot accept both as equally divine forces. They are inclined to agree with Luther in some of his statements and with the Anabaptists in holding a low estimate of the worth of the state. If God is related to the state, it is only in the vague and remote sense that everything ultimately is dependent upon God. On the other hand, some with more dualistic tendencies are ready to ascribe the founding of the state to Satan and the founding of the church to God. Thus, the opposition between church and state is more than a parallelism and, indeed, more than a paradox.

In this view, the state is clearly of less value, while the church represents the direct activities of God in the world.

The state represents the unredeemed of humanity; the church represents those who have experienced God's salvation. This may be taken to mean that those who advocate the dominance of the church over the state believe in the radical nature of sin. They do not believe that unredeemed humanity is capable of establishing holy commonwealths, free from the taint of sin. For Christians to participate in the affairs of the state, as Luther once suggested, with concern for others rather than self and for the achievement of the social principle of love, is not only rationally indefensible but spiritually delusory. The choice must be made, it is claimed, and both the high teachings of religion and social experience itself conclude that the church is superior to the state.

Clement of Alexandria supported this view, but it was Thomas Aquinas who not only expounded it systematically and related the superiority of the church to all phases of medieval society, but who has had a lasting influence in maintaining this view in the succeeding centuries.

Ambrose

Again, the view of the dominance of the church over the state is more than a theory. Many instances of its concrete expression in Western civilization could be recounted. Ambrose provides a case study of this type. Born in western Germany in the fourth century, educated in Rome for a civil career, and a governor of a large part of northern Italy, he found himself elected Bishop of Milan. Soon thereafter an influential group in Rome sought to persuade Valentinian II to restore the altar of victory in the Senate chamber and to reinstate other practices of the older, non-Christian religion. Ambrose opposed these efforts and finally persuaded Valentinian to deny the requests.

Ambrose again demonstrated the dominance of the church over the state when Valentinian, angered by the assassination of the governor of Thessalonica in 390, instituted a massacre of that city's inhabitants. Ambrose was appalled, as were others. He called upon the Emperor to admit his mistake through public repentance. Valentinian obeyed.

Gregory

Gregory the Great (540-604), who along with Ambrose, Augustine, and Jerome is termed the Doctors of the Latin church, provides another example of the ability of the church to dominate the state. Born in Rome of a senatorial Christian family, he was appointed governor of that city in 573 by Emperor Justin II. The appeal of the monastic life took him from service to the state for a time, but later he was appointed by Pope Pelagius II (579-590) as papal ambassador to the court of Constantinople. In 590, as the first monk to attain that office, Gregory was chosen pope. Even before this time, the state in Italy had been weakened by the Lombards, who threatened Rome itself. It was Gregory, however, rather than the emperor, who became the outstanding leader against Lombard aggression. He defended Rome by force and by tribute, raising troops to fend off the invaders, and finally even made peace with the Lombards on his own authority. In effect, he was both pope and sovereign, demonstrating the ability of the church to dominate the state.

John Calvin

One of the most significant examples in Western history of church dominance over the state is the experience of John Calvin in Geneva. Although Calvin was never ordained, he did study philosophy and dialectics at the University of Paris. Largely as a consequence of involvement in Reformation activities, he left the university in 1535 to seek safety in Protestant Basel. In an effort to defend fellow believers, he wrote his *Institutes of the Christian Religion,* prefacing it with a letter to the French king. This letter, if not the longer document, put him at the forefront of French Protestantism. Calvin was not an essentially creative or original thinker, but he selectively and effectively deployed ideas secured from Luther, Butzer, and others. His task was basically that of formulation and systematic presentation.

Calvin also differed from his mentors. One of these differences laid the basis for his ideas on the social consequences of the church. Agreeing with Luther, Calvin taught that salvation is secured by faith, rather than by works, but he also taught that the believer is characterized by works pleasing to God and that such works constitute the proof that the believer has entered into vital union with Christ. Said Calvin: "We are justified not without, and yet not by works." Thus, his doctrine of "good works" laid a basis for his idea that the Christian possesses social responsibilities.

Through a set of circumstances beyond his control, a political party instigated a political revolution in Geneva. With difficulty, the party persuaded him in 1541 to return to

Geneva from Strasbourg. Upon his return he secured the adoption of his new ecclesiastical constitution, the *Ordonnances*, which declared that Christ had instituted in the church the four offices of pastor, teacher, elder, and deacon. The pastors were to be available for public discussion, examination of ministerial candidates, and the exposition of the faith. The teacher became the head of the Geneva school system, fulfilling a cardinal tenet in Calvin's thinking: that religious training should be provided for all of the citizens. The deacons were assigned the care of the poor and the supervision of hospitals.

The heart of Calvin's *Ordonnances*, however, was the elders. The elders were laymen, chosen by the Little Council. Together with the ministers, they made up the Consistory, which met every Thursday and was responsible for ecclesiastical discipline. The Consistory possessed significant religious and secular power, including the right of excommunication, but the civil authorities also were involved in the application of certain of the serious penalties. It must be noted, moreover, that while Calvin favored the establishment of a church-state, one in which the church dominated the state, he believed that the church alone should be responsible for excommunication.

The dominance of the church over the state in Calvin's Geneva is further illustrated by the actions taken against Jerome Hermes Bolsec and Michael Servetus. Bolsec, a former monk from Paris, asserted that Calvin's doctrine of predestination was in error. Calvin took Bolsec's charges before the city government in the fall of 1551, and a trial was held. Bolsec was banished. Servetus published his *De Trinitatis Erroribus* in 1531; in it he criticized the Nicene doctrine of the Trinity, the Chalcedonian Christology, and infant baptism. He was arrested in Geneva in August, 1553, tried, convicted, and put to death by fire on October 27, 1553.

Calvin's theological conceptions and his view of the dominance of the church over the state continued long after his death, and spread in one form or another to many parts of the Western world. In the English and American experience, for example, Calvinism was expressed mainly in Puritanism. To Max Weber, Puritanism is one of the two "solutions" that are consistent with the universalist views of religion (in this case, the world's religions) in their efforts to counteract the claims of the state. Says Weber:

Puritanism, with its particularism of grace and vocational asceticism, believes in the fixed and revealed commandments of a God who is otherwise quite incomprehensible. It interprets God's will to mean that these commandments should be imposed upon the creatural world by the means of this world, namely, violence—for the world is subject to violence and ethical barbarism.[16]

TRANSFORMATIONISM

Transformationism is the final form which the relations between church and state may take. Like the three preceding forms, it, too, appears to be dependent upon the types of identity and parallelism. It is placed last in the typology because it is composed of ingredients that characterize all of the other types, with the possible exception of that involving state dominance over the church. It is closest to church dominance over the state. To this category, H. Richard Niebuhr applies the term "conversionist." [17]

Transformationism lays stress upon the continuing activity of God in creation. It shuns the notion that God's creation is finished or that he is not actively at work in all aspects of nature, man, and society. Because God is active in all aspects of his creation, there is always the possibility that all aspects of the creation will undergo the redemption which in the Christian faith is provided to believers. The transformationist both delights in the acknowledged achievements of man in his participation in the several social institutions, excluding the church, and yet realizes that all expressions of the given order of things are lacking in the desired perfection. He looks to some combination of the efforts of God and himself, both as an individual and as a participant in society's affairs, as the potential agent of human betterment. He is a religious meliorist.

To some extent the transformationist holds views similar to the views of those who advocate paradoxism. He believes that God expresses his responsibility to the whole of creation, both church and state, and that the state, without the expressed grace of God evident in the church, operates both despite and in fulfillment of the will of God. Transformationism, moreover, is not doctrinaire in its acceptance of the oppositional nature of the state to the church and to the will of God. On the other hand, it asserts the clear superiority of the principles and practices that guide the church and considers the church as the social institution which possesses the resources necessary for the ultimate redemption of the state and the other social institutions in society. Yet in principle transformationism does not favor the dominance of the church over the state, but advocates the usefulness of both institutions interacting.

Social historians are not agreed on specific historical examples of transformationism. H. Richard Niebuhr, for example, thinks that "conversionism" is founded in the Gospel of John, and that it is taught by Augustine, Calvin, and such modern thinkers as Jonathan Edwards and F. D. Maurice.[18] Thomas G. Sanders believes that transformationism originated in its developed form in Calvinism, the English Puritans, the theocracy of the Massachusetts Bay colony, and in such modern figures as Lyman Beecher and Walter Rauschenbusch. It is clear, however, that transformationism both past and present is a vital option for church-state relations.

7

Non-Christian Religions
and the State

NEW OPENNESS

The new openness on the part of the churches regarding
their place in relation to the religions of mankind provides
a suitable context in which the relations of church and
state may be studied beyond even the scope of Christianity. An illustration of this new openness is the establishment by Pope Paul VI in May, 1964, of the Vatican
Secretariat for Non-Christians, whose task is that of maintaining relations with all of the world's religions not based
on the divinity of Jesus Christ. The new secretariat
parallels the Secretariat for Christian Unity, which seeks
points of contact among Roman Catholics and other Christians. The pope, explaining his hope in establishing the
new secretariat, said, "No pilgrim, no matter how far,
religiously and geographically, may be the country from
which he comes, will be any longer a stranger in this
Rome. . . ."[1]

But the new openness is based upon a long history of
interest within the churches in the nature and meaning of

the non-Christian religions. Mircea Eliade provides a chronological survey of the history of religion as a branch of knowledge, pointing out, for example, that the first university chair of the history of religion was founded in Geneva in 1873, and in 1876 four such chairs were established in Holland. Even so, interest in the non-Christian religions predates the founding of these professorships by several centuries.[2] Recent years have brought about an expansion of this interest, with an accompanying extension of the available literature.[3]

SOME PROBLEMS OF COMPARISON

Superficially viewed, all religions appear to possess a common character. The features of one seem to have their parallels in the other religions. Such general and hasty observations have been made by many untrained persons, who assume that all of man's religions are highly similar, if not identical, even though the language used to describe the particular content is distinctive.

But a more specialized analysis of man's religions indicates that not only are the languages different, but the forms often are dissimilar and distinctive. Comparisons may validly be made, but identities are to be most carefully avoided. Each religion is a complex social phenomenon unto itself and is as unique as a human fingerprint. The distinctiveness of the religions of man is nowhere more apparent than in their teachings on the subject of church and state.

The church, for example, bears a relationship to the concept of the community, yet it is a convened or enacted community, rather than a "natural community." The church in this sense is not identifiable with those religious groupings of mankind in which the sacred community is coterminous with the secular community.

The church, again, represents a chosen people who live in a covenanted relationship to God, but this covenanted relationship is extended universally and does not depend upon a unique relationship to a people of a nation, as in Judaism.

In these and other ways, then, the church appears to be a social phenomenon distinctive to Christianity. A similar conclusion is drawn by G. van Der Leeuw, who states:

A church actually exists solely in Christianity; for neither the Buddhist monastic community, nor that of Islam resting on the principle of mere agreement and conformity, nor again the Judaic assembly of the people, merits the title of church. This historic fact, still further, is intimately connected with the church's essential nature, since it arose from the concrete historical situation in which the Jews' rejection of Christ, and the subsequent turning towards the heathen, brought in their train. In this concrete situation, then, there subsists on the one hand the transition from community to covenant, but on the other, the concentration of the heathen religious consciousness, already manifested in various types of covenant, into a community given in a new manner. Thus, the church is the church of the heathen, but "salvation is of the Jews." [4]

Yet to make such a claim regarding the church is not to conclude that the church as a social institution is superior to all other religious forms (except perhaps to the claim of Christian faith). It is simply different. To make such a claim, moreover, is not to hold that both natural and specially enacted forms of religious community are not present in the non-Christian religions, for every religion possesses some kind of social consciousness which results in a social form that maintains and expresses this consciousness.

Religion is often tied to natural human groups. Joachim Wach, for example, has identified and elaborated the following forms of natural and religious grouping: (1) family cults, (2) kinship cults, (3) local cults, (4) racial cults, (5) national cults, and (6) cult associations based on sex and age.[5] The ties between religion and natural groups create a strong cohesion between them. All actions on the part of the natural groups are closely related to those of their religion. Similarly, all acts of a religious nature strengthen the integration already evident in the naturalness (based on relations by blood or by marriage) already in existence. Both the social and the religious aspects of the integration of natural groups are responsive to change from a variety of directions in the culture, making integration a dynamic rather than a static characteristic. Obviously, however, those religious formations which are based upon an identity with natural groups are not to be equated with the church, as it is understood in the Christian tradition, since the church transcends all natural groupings.

Religion is also related to the specifically religious or enacted organization of society. In these forms, some degree of separation is achieved between the enacted organization and the other social institutions in society. The specifically religious organizations are formed for distinctively religious purposes, although they may also contribute to social cohesion. On this score, Wach discusses a multiplicity of enacted forms, such as (1) the secret society; (2) the mystery society, like those of Greece and Rome; (3) the *Sampradaya* of Hinduism; (4) the founded religion (including the circle of disciples, the brotherhood, and the ecclesiastical body), and (5) the groups formed through reaction and protest (involving individual and collective types of protest, especially those within the religious organization, and those which have resulted in secession).[6] Of all of these types, however, Wach concludes that "the ecclesiastical body" as found in such non-Christian religions as Judaism, Confucianism, Islam, and Buddhism, comes closest to what Christians mean by the term "church." But, he claims, "ecclesiastical bodies may resemble one another in many respects structurally, but they differ considerably in their self-interpretation, in theology, in soteriology, and eschatology." He notes that from a theological point of view "there can be only one Christian church even though broken up into a number of bodies, each claiming the—exclusive —right to represent the whole as well as the ideal." [7]

On the basis of the evidence presented, it seems reasonable to conclude that the relationship of church and state as understood within the context of those historical situations in which the Christian Church has been related to various historical forms of the state is a phenomenon distinctive to Christianity and these states. The non-Christian religions have held a variety of relationships, both generally and specifically, with the states with which they have been involved. However, these cannot be naïvely equated with those involving Christianity, and must be understood in their own right and not on the basis of either identity or analogy with the Christian understanding of church-state relations.

FOUR TYPES OF RELATIONSHIPS

Employing a methodology similar to that of H. Richard Niebuhr in his typology of the relations of "Christ and culture," it may be possible to speak of the general relationships between the non-Christian religions and the societies in which they are maintained and nourished.[8] Such a typology, as is true of Niebuhr's, claims to be suggestive, rather than one that establishes exclusive categories. As will be seen, most if not all of the religions, because of their great complexity, fall into more than one type. The categories, moreover, refer to the ethos of the religions rather than to any or all of their organizational, cultic, or doctrinal manifestations.

Bearing in mind these qualifications, the following four types of relationships are observed between the non-Christian religions and their societies: (1) religions of a people, (2) religions closely supportive of a people, (3) religions of withdrawal, and (4) religions of universal scope. This typology is based upon the assumption that some religions are practically identifiable with the people of a society or nation; that other religions are not so closely identified, but are mainly committed to the social values which are held at large among a people; that other religions tend to view themselves as somewhat separate from their surrounding cultures; and that religions of universal scope are faced with essentially different and distinctive circumstances.

A brief and admittedly superficial review of some of the religions of mankind by means of this typology will, it is hoped, provide perspective from which the distinctiveness of church-state relations within Christianity may be appreciated.

Religions of a People

Certain religions, such as Shintoism, Judaism, Hinduism, Sikhism, and Confucianism, are largely religions of a people. Historically, they have been relatively bound to the territories of a particular population and have not, in the main, claimed to be universal in scope. They have not only been strongly supportive of their surrounding cultures, but to a significant degree have been identified with them. They may support the distinction between the social institutions of religion and the state, but they perceive them to be completely harmonious because the goals are almost completely identical.

Shintoism is a prime example of a religion of a people.[9] As the immemorial national religion of Japan, Shintoism historically has made significant contributions to the political theory and the national stability of the Japanese nation. In a sense, it is more of a patriotic cult than it is a religion. Since its fundamental requirement is that of political loyalty, it provides a formal basis of social cohesion for the Japanese people.

According to Shinto teachings, the islands of Japan were the first creation of the sun goddess, Ama-terasu, who even today is the most important among the nature deities of Shintoism. Shintoism also holds that the first emperor, or mikado, was a literal descendant from the sun goddess. Thus, the sanctity of the Japanese people is assured by Shintoism from the time of the creation of the universe. Until after the Second World War, every emperor was considered a direct descendant of the sun goddess and, therefore, worthy of reverence and worship.

After 1889, however, the Japanese government distinguished between state Shintoism and sectarian Shintoism. The government maintained that the Shintoism carried on at the state shrines constituted a form of patriotism, while that conducted at sectarian shrines was wholly elective and voluntary. The government supported the state shrines, while voluntary contributions supported the latter. The administration of state Shintoism was vested in the Bureau of Shrines in the Department of Home Affairs, a part of the national government.

After 1945, and as a consequence of the American occupation, state Shintoism was disestablished. Today Shintoism is managed in the Bureau of Religion within the Department of Education, along with Buddhism, Christianity, and other religions. No state official, including the emperor, may now participate in any Shinto ceremonial in an official capacity. While at first this disestablishment caused widespread confusion among the Japanese people, in recent years there has been a renewal of sectarian Shintoism and a generally constructive adaptation of the old religion to new official requirements.

Historically, Shintoism has been the singular religion of the Japanese people, and even today constitutes a faith which the vast majority of the Japanese find congenial to their outlook on life.

Other religions also may be classified as religions of a people. In this sense, Judaism has been historically bound to the people called the Jews. The Jews, as explained in Chapter 4, were covenanted people, people who were chosen by God to bear a unique relationship to him. This covenant was not one between individuals and God, but between the corporate membership of Hebrew society and God. To belong to God meant that the people was bound by the exclusive relationship, that their religion and their existence as a nation were coterminous.

The sacred scriptures of Judaism are reserved to the recounting in various styles of the "mighty acts of God" in his relations with the Jewish people. The social ethics enjoined by Judaism on its followers were not simply a consequence of social consensus or the leadership of wise individuals only, but were, as the prophets indicated, the transcendental requirements of a holy and righteous God. While God in Judaism is the God of all peoples, he is specially concerned with the welfare of his chosen people and calls them, in a wilderness of low morality, to standards of high ethical import.

Judaism, however, has had its relationship to the chosen people disturbed by several events, such as the exile in Babylonia, the Diaspora, and the present scattering of the people throughout the world, despite the fact that Israel, the modern Jewish state, is a haven for many.

Sikhism, whose followers in India numbered slightly more than six million in 1951, also may be said to be a religion of a people. Although Sikhism originally sought to combine the best elements of Hinduism and Islam, it became in fact a separate and independent religion. Of it, Robert E. Hume has written:

Politically, Sikhism is the only religion in the history of the world which has given birth to a nation, with the exception of Judaism. Its chief place in history has been political more than religious. In its case, as also is the case of Judaism, political independence has been destroyed, while religiously and every other wise, the people have continued strikingly able and distinctive.[10]

The political aspirations of the Sikhs were recognized by the government of India in 1966 when a separate Sikh state was established in the Punjab.

At times, as in the religions cited, the top officials of the religious organization are also the top officials of the government, being revered either as gods or as divinely appointed persons.

Those non-Christian religions which are the religions of a people appear, with notable exceptions, to experience little tension or conflict between the social institutions of religion and government. Religion of this kind is a powerful means of maintaining the dominant values of the people. Both religion and government work hand in hand, each tending to strengthen the other.

Religions Closely Supportive of a People

Among the religions of mankind are some which are closely supportive of the dominant and avowedly non-religious values of their surrounding cultures. Religions of this sort are not dissimilar from religions of a people, except that they may not hold an exclusive relationship to the people or possess a genuinely official sanction for their supporting relationship. Quite possibly in this category are Confucianism, Hinduism, and Taoism. Each of the major religions, however, possesses teachers and tendencies which are classifiable in more than one category.

Confucianism, like Shintoism and some other religions, is thought by some not to be a religion at all. Rather, it is considered to be an ethical code or social philosophy. Confucius, for example, showed little concern with such traditional features of religion as prayer, the afterlife, and God. Confucius was not the autonomous originator of Confucianism, since the Chinese people had been practicing the precepts which he enunciated many centuries before his time. Also, he himself made no claim to be an innovator. In fact, he was not concerned with new things, but with the past. He sought to codify those ethical principles which he and the people of his time had inherited, to stamp his personality upon them, and to make more possible their embodiment in the social life of China.

Of primary concern to Confucius were the so-called five relations: (1) of ruler and subject, (2) of father and son, (3) of husband and wife, (4) of elder brother and younger brother, and (5) of friend and friend. Filial piety was the chief virtue in Confucianism, and this ideal has had an important historical impact upon the total life of the Chinese people. The individual was enjoined to become a superior man. Being a superior man meant living at one's best in every concrete situation.

In addition, Confucius, while he did not stress the future life, did advocate ancestor worship. Aside from its doctrinal implications, stress upon this belief tended to be a conserving and integrating force in Chinese life. Whatever had been, was accepted and even revered. The authority of the past, handed down from generation to generation, became the guideline for action in the present. The manner in which Confucianism contributed, in the original teachings of the founder and in the subsequent modifications and developments of the religion, to the social life of China is witnessed to by almost every learned observer. Of course, the founding of the Republic of China in 1915 made major changes in the relationship of Confucianism to its surrounding culture, and the dominance of political communism following the Second World War has also had significant effects. But historically, and to some extent even today, Confucianism may be classified as a religion which is mainly supportive of its surrounding culture.

Hinduism is a religion which is closely supportive of Indian culture, although in its long history it has been so varied and even contradictory that almost any generalization can be countered by another. However, despite its variations, Hinduism is closely allied with the historic social system of India. The religion was the main support for the caste system, in which there were four main castes and hundreds or even thousands of mutually exclusive subcastes. According to this system, conceived by Hinduism to be divinely appointed, the members of the castes must follow their hereditary occupations and must refrain from marrying, eating, and, in some instances, socializing with members of other castes. A fifth major grouping, the "untouchables," fell into a distinct category. Post-colonial India, following its Constitution of 1948, is officially a secular nation. The fact remains, however, that Hinduism, experiencing a recent revival, constitutes the ethos of the Indian people. It is by Hinduism's treasure of ancient teachings and practices that modern Hindus today are guided.

In religions that are mainly supportive of their surrounding culture, there also is little ground for tensions and conflicts between religion and government. The essential task of religion is that of furthering the maintenance and enrichment of the social values of the society. The primary responsibility of the state is to act according to the tradition-received values inherent in religion. While both religion and the government may be viewed as separate institutions, they are commingled in their functions and goals.

Religions of Withdrawal

The third type of relationship that exists in the non-Christian religions is exemplified by the religions of withdrawal, which commonly are not official religions. They do not find it possible to support the dominant culture that surrounds them. They are schismatic in that they draw a sharp line between what the culture enjoins and what is necessary for salvation. In general, they tend to be the religions of minorities within societies in which the majorities accept a culture-supporting religion.

The religions of withdrawal, however, may not remain as minority religions—as was the case of Buddhism. While Buddhism stressed asceticism in its early stages and called for withdrawal from society, it rapidly modified these original features as it spread throughout India and much of the rest of Asia. As Buddhism developed, compromising as it did with its originally pure doctrine of asceticism, it grew through two main branches. Hinayana Buddhism, the "Lesser Vehicle," found mainly in southern Asia, maintained the viewpoint that speculative religion is profitless, that society is essentially evil, and that salvation is secured through the absence of passion, quiescence, and striving for Nirvana. Mahayana Buddhism, the "Greater Vehicle," found mainly in China and Japan, developed as a full-fledged religion with beliefs and practices that are not found in the life and teachings of the religion's founder.

Among the religions of the third type are, wholly or partly, Jainism, Buddhism, Hinduism, Taoism, and Zoroastrianism.

Jainism was founded by Mahavira in the sixth century B.C. Although the founder was born to luxury, he withdrew from the world upon the death of his parents, joining a body of monks. Later, going out on his own, he wandered through the villages of central India, seeking release from the cycle of birth, death, and rebirth. Two beliefs dominated his outlook: first, that the severest asceticism was necessary for the purging of contaminating matter from the soul and, second, that *ahimsa,* noninjury to living beings, was a necessary part of the practice of the ascetic life. Mahavira's doctrine of asceticism rested upon the essential opposition of matter and mind, soul and flesh. Matter and the flesh are evil; the mind and the soul are good. Matter and the flesh need to be resisted and annihilated, in order that the mind and the soul may be released from restrictions and may develop in their purity. These teachings of ascetic practice were summarized in the "Five Great Vows" for the monk-followers of Mahavira. Even sex interest was renounced.

It is interesting to note that Jain sects are divided primarily on the matter of the appropriate degree of asceticism to be followed. The Shvetambaras, "the white-clad," are those who wear at least one garment. The Digambaras, those "clad in atmosphere," do not wear clothes, claiming that even Mahavira did not dress. A third sect, the Sthanakvasis, do not believe in houses of worship, and detest idols. They claim that Jainism can be practiced everywhere through personal discipline.

The Jains, who now number only about two million and are found mostly around Bombay, India, have never claimed to represent the dominant culture of India. They have stood aloof from it, proclaiming that the way of salvation demands that the individual withdraw from society, in order that he may concentrate upon the virtues of the spirit while subduing the evils of matter.

Zoroastrianism holds a view of reality which is similar (though not identical) to that of Jainism. Reality, from the standpoint of deity, is truncated. The one supreme deity in Zoroastrianism is Ahura Mazda, the power of light, truth, life, and goodness. But there also is Angra Mainyu, a demon or deity who is the incarnation of all known evil. Thus, a fundamentally cosmological dualism exists in Zoroastrianism. The world and everything in it represent the interplay of two battling cosmic powers who are relatively coequal from the beginning of time. Like Jainism, Zoroastrianism favors the higher principle of light (mind); it resists and despises the lower principle of darkness (matter). The practical social consequences of the theological foundation of Zoroastrianism call for the support of the good. Although strict asceticism is not enjoined, the follower is called upon to be a faithful and charitable person, knowing the good and always fighting the evil, even as Ahura Mazda does.

The social consequences of Zoroastrianism led to a lack of full and complete indentification of the religion with its surrounding culture. The decisive break between good and evil in the theological aspects of the religion impelled it to assert the primacy of the higher values. Zoroastrianism encourages at least a partial withdrawal from the dominant values of society. Thus, it is an example of the third type of relationship between religion and culture.

Taoism, the religion founded by Lao-tze in the sixth century B.C. in China, is not based upon the dualism of good and evil, but it is essentially a religion of social withdrawal. It calls upon the individual to follow the way (Tao), this way involving quiet, rest, and simplicity in living. The placid, self-contented indifferent person is the one who is most virtuous in Taoism. Very little evil exists in the world, according to this religion, and there appears to be no need for a cosmological explanation of evil. No supreme and personal God exists, nor does a personal Devil, and man is not caught in the dilemma of the dualism as taught by Jainism and Zoroastrianism. Similarly, no social program of salvation is required, and the individual is enjoined to be quiet and simple in his living. Because of its nature, as Joachim Wach remarks: ". . . Taoism never succeeded in overcoming the suspicion and even the oppression of its native state in spite of the patronage of some individual rulers." [11]

The religions of withdrawal have generally maintained a degree of separateness from the rest of society, including the government. They are based upon the availability of a principle for the guidance of life that is superior to the one which is available to the masses of the people. Such religions tend to take refuge in monastic orders and ascetic practices. They may or may not be in actual conflict with the state, as is evidenced by the fact that Asoka was the Buddhist ruler of India and apparently found no contradiction in his two roles. Again, Ardeshir I, an active adherent of Zoroastrianism, was able in the third century B.C. to establish Persia's independence, founding the Sassanian dynasty. In the main, however, the religions of withdrawal have been tolerated by the governments under which they existed.

Religions of Universal Scope

The fourth and final type of relationship is that which characterizes the non-Christian religions of universal scope, in which category, it is commonly agreed, are Buddhism and Islam. (Christianity is, of course, also a religion of universal scope.)

There is a sense in which other religions were or sought to be universal. Jainism originally had tendencies to become a universal religion, although these were never fulfilled. Zoroastrianism in the fifth and sixth centuries B.C. was spread by conquering armies over Babylonia and pushed on into Europe until stopped at the battle of Salamis (480 B.C.). After many years of such struggles, however, Zoroastrianism became restricted mainly to a section of India, where its adherents are known as Parsees.

Buddhism and Islam are religions of universal scope, although their history and present geographic spread clearly indicate that they have developed unevenly throughout the world. Buddhism is dominant mainly in Asia; Islam flourishes mainly in the Middle East and certain parts of Africa and Pakistan. In this sense, they may be thought of as "world-regional religions," but their intended scope is universal. They declare themselves not to be respecters of national boundaries or of particular races, ethnic heritages, political forms, and other manifestations of parochialism.

The existence of a religion of universal scope is the basis of great wonder and mystery. Wach asserts: "The emergence of any great new religious faith is one of the inexplicable mysteries which have accompanied the ascent of man and bears the most convincing testimony to the contingency and spontaneity of his spiritual history." [12] But the emergence of a religion of universal scope is an even greater mystery and cause for amazement.

Each of the three universal religions began as a minority faith in one culture. Each was formed as a schism from an existing religion. Buddhism, like Jainism, began as an ascetic revolt against the worldly excesses of Hinduism. Islam originated as a creative protest against the naturalistic religion of the people of the Arabian Peninsula. Each received acceptance, rejection, and indifference from the surrounding culture as well as from those who held political power. At one time or another, each also became a state religion, although each is now found in nations of the world where the secular state is the ideal or where some other religion is the official one.

The religions of universal scope also express some degree of alienation from any and all cultures in which they have been found. Each has laid claim to being the religion of all mankind, and as a consequence each cannot be identified with any particular culture or any particular nation. Each has been found to exist and flourish in nations which feature highly different and even opposed types of government. Probably a high degree of cultural alienation is necessary for any religion which seeks to attain universal scope. From this standpoint, the question is not what is the proper relationship of church and state, but what is the proper relationship of the church to the states.

Since the religions of universal scope are alienated to a degree from their surrounding cultures, they also may be more prone to develop extensive self definitions through international councils and organizations. Such efforts are necessary for the maintenance of the supranational character of the religions. These religions need defensively to be concerned with their own natures in order to maintain their coherence in the face of a "multiverse" of cultural pressures.

The religions of universal scope, moreover, resting minimally upon ties to natural groupings, need to be based upon the intensified religious experience of individuals. Thus, individualism may be the creation (even in the face of authoritarian governments) of a religious necessity for identification with the universal values as embodied in a religion of universal scope. Morroe Berger has come to this conclusion in the case of Islam:

Is there a real contradiction between two characteristics of Near Eastern political life we have pointed out—individualism, hostility to government, and a passion for equality on one side, and despotic governments making broad claims on the other? I think not. Individualism among Arab Moslems is not a political trait; it refers to equality of social status, individual freedom to follow the way of the Prophet, which have been jealously guarded.[13]

So, too, with Buddhism. In Buddhism the adherent seeks Nirvana, not through the intercession of international organizations founded to define and expand Buddhism, but through the individual questing of the person in his solitariness.

Recently, standing in stark contrast with much of Buddhism's historical stress upon individualism and withdrawal from society, is the militant Soka Gakkai sect in Japan. Led by piously political Daisaku Ikeda, Soka Gakkai (Value-Creation Society) has attracted youthful Japanese city dwellers, who have lost contact with the ward-oriented politics of their rural home towns, through the society's political arm, the Komeito, the Clean Government Party. Early in 1967 the Komeito captured twenty-five seats in Japan's tenth postwar election. Now the third strongest party in Japanese politics, the burgeoning, Buddhist-backed Komeito appears to be establishing a new relationship between Buddhism and government.[14]

Individualism in Christianity, however, seems to be

related to the realization of Christianity in its modern social and national forms, following the breakdown of the corporateness of the church's life in the medieval period, and with the growth of increasingly centralized and powerful states which by themselves have been able to maintain social cohesion.

The relations of church and state as experienced in Western and nominally Christian civilization, then, appear to be different from those of religions of a people, religions closely supportive of the culture of a people, and religions of withdrawal. The relations of church and state in the Western tradition have been similar to, but not identical with, those of the other religions of universal scope: Buddhism and Islam. Yet despite all of the similarities and exceptions, the relations of church and state cannot be satisfactorily resolved by seeking to imitate the experience of the non-Christian religions. They can be resolved, if ever, only by faithfully following the implications for the relations that are found in our own religious and cultural traditions.

But the relations of church and state in the so-called Christian West are currently being modified by a variety of factors. For example, the development of missions to North America and Europe on the part of Hindu, Buddhist, and Muslim reform movements has introduced new insights into the situation confronting Americans. Another factor which is modifying the current situation is the slow but steady growth of a world culture. On this score, Michael Novak says:

. . . human actions have, unlike liturgy, a social context. In the world in which we are coming to live, this context embraces all men: One's neighbor is the Viet Cong, the Russian, the Harlemite, or the Nob Hill matron. Christianity offers no escape from the complexities and ambiguities of the new world culture; nor does it offer (as Judaeo-Christian culture often did) a complacent satisfaction that one has all, or even any complete answers.[15]

8

The Church and Totalitarianism

ORIGIN

In the course of human history, totalitarianism has been both praised and anathematized. Plato, for example, commended the virtuous tyrant, believing that such a figure is politically necessary in order to insure human welfare. In his *Laws* Plato advocates the extreme of thought control by "the interpreter of the law." In regard to the youth, Plato asserted that those who disobeyed the properly held views of the virtuous tyrant should be brought before the court and, if found guilty, placed by the judge in a House of Reformation for not less than five years. Anyone, upon release, who continues in his "impiety" and is condemned a second time, "let him be punished with death."

Even in modern times, however, dictatorships have been praised. From history's perspective it may seem strange, but nevertheless it is true, that Sidney and Beatrice Webb argued in *The Truth About Soviet Russia* that Stalin was not a dictator, but a great democrat who brought political and economic democracy to Russia.[1] Even Adolph Hitler evoked psalms of praise from many both within Germany and, what is worse, elsewhere.

But, in general, totalitarianism has been viewed as a

curse upon mankind. Not an affliction solely characteristic of the past, totalitarianism is viewed today as a scourge and a serious threat. Thus Hannah Arendt, in writing on the origin of totalitarianism, notes "the profound upheavals of our time." She asserts that this period of history is experiencing "perhaps the most profound crisis in Western history since the downfall of the Roman Empire." [2] Similarly, George F. Kennan soberly considers totalitarianism to be

. . . a phenomenon of our time that has brought the deepest possible misery to untold millions of our contemporaries, even to the point of rendering life itself a hated burden to them. As a source of sorrow and suffering to the human race, I suppose this phenomenon has overshadowed every other source of human woe in our time; for it has demeaned humanity in its own sight, attacked man's confidence in himself, made him realize that he can be his own most terrible and dangerous enemy, more bestial than the beasts, more cruel than nature.[3]

The impact of totalitarianism upon the churches has had far-reaching consequences in the past and at present. Totalitarianism as a theory of the state constitutes a formidable problem of modern times, from the standpoint of the churches, and therefore constitutes an appropriate subject for this chapter.

Rise of National States

The Middle Ages was a remarkable period in human history, by any account. Among its significant features was the continuous tension which existed between religious and secular authorities and the gradual development of national states. Between 1050 and 1300 the kings and popes in Europe seemed to be in one continuous crisis. The kings, varying in their theory and practice, asserted their pre-eminence in government and at times even aspired to combine supreme temporal power with supreme spiritual power by, for example, appointing bishops and, in other instances, even claiming to depose popes. The popes, on the other hand, both in theory and in practice, regularly held that they were God's chief representatives on earth —Christ's vicars—who held the keys that could bind or loose all things on earth. Both kings and popes appealed to selected Biblical texts and to the writings of the early Fathers of the Church. In fact, during the course of centuries some of the rulers of Sicily, Sardinia, Corsica, Aragon, Hungary, and Dalmatia readily looked to the pope as a feudal overlord who could protect them against territorially hungry competitors. The situation for centuries was greatly confused, and resulted in open humiliation and conflict on numerous occasions.

The consequences of the tension between kings and popes were many. An important body of literature was developed over the centuries which defined the nature of the church, especially the organizational church, to a degree that had not been known. The consequence of this massive development of doctrine upon the nature of the church is a heritage which influences thinkers to the present day. Another consequence was the development of the idea of the state itself; Western constitutionalism is a direct result of the elaboration of doctrines regarding the nature of the state that were developed in the Middle Ages. In addition, a series of concrete historical developments brought about the new national powers. In France, England, Spain, and to some degree in Germany, the development of national states became a reality in which the independence and autonomy of the rulers were not only affirmed but firmly maintained. As Williston Walker states: "The half-century from 1450 to 1500 saw a remarkable growth in royal authority and national consciousness in the western kingdoms of Europe." [4]

Rise of Secular States

The rise of national states is a factor of great significance for all later forms of the state, since they asserted an authority that, at least in practice, was not subservient to the church. They were, in essence, secular states. They reflected the shift in cultural ethos that had been taking place during the very time in which national sovereignties were developed in Europe. Many factors account for this change. The Holy Roman Empire disappeared. The Enlightenment, with its skepticism, laid the foundations for later rationalism and science. The Reformation increased churchly diversity and established new spheres of political influence. The right of the church to control education and marriages came under critical review. The new nations united Protestant and Catholic regions into one state, thus leading in some instances to the acceptance of the principle of toleration of religious differences. The papacy, moreover, assuming the futility of contesting the temporal supremacy of national rulers, began to develop a new status with various states by negotiating concordats. These and other factors led not only to the growth of secular states, but also of secular society. A Roman Catholic theologian summarized this process of secularization thus:

During the middle ages the ecclesiastical institution included and formed human societies; but from the beginning of the fourteenth century society began slowly to assert its independence. First to cut loose were rulers and their politics, then various activities of urban life and welfare, then thought and the sciences, the morality and spirituality itself, finally, and much more radically, the common consciousness of the people in their daily life of sorrows, joys, hope.[5]

The "crisis of church and state" that existed from 1050 to 1300 was dissolved with the growth of secular national states.[6] The rise of the independent sovereign state, moreover, laid the basis for totalitarianism in at least two ways. First, it rejected the controlling requirements of ethical and spiritual realities, whether these were recognized as organized in institutional forms or not. The Roman Catholic Church and the claims of the Christian faith itself were assumed not to be superior to national sovereignty. Second, the secularized national state became for some, often the elite who were the rulers, an end in itself:

It is presumed in modern international law that if a state is an independent sovereign state, there can be no authority over it, that it can submit to no obligations which could be regarded as binding its will. A state may of course undertake obligations, subscribe to covenants and sign treaties. But it may, on this theory, repudiate such obligations if it will. It always retains its power of decision. A state is not, and on this theory cannot be, a member of a wider community bound by law as is the citizen of a state.[7]

Preconditions

Most authorities are agreed that the rise of modern totalitarianism did not result solely from the division of authority between the social institutions of church and state, although they are not agreed as to the nature and number of the preconditions that led to the totalitarian states of recent history. Obviously, not all secular, sovereign states have become totalitarian. What other factors, then, might be at work in the establishment of totalitarianism? A number of suggested answers have been provided. Hannah Arendt, for example, shows in a lengthy study that the roots of totalitarianism grew out of the political and nationalistic situation in the nineteenth century. She presents a vivid account of the Dreyfus affair as a "kind of dress rehearsal for the performance of our time." The "Period of Imperialism," between 1884 and the outbreak of the First World War, also is considered by Dr. Arendt as a further preparation for totalitarianism. These two elements, then, anti-Semitism and imperialism, are the preconditions of totalitarianism.[8]

Carl J. Friedrich suggests three preconditions which do not include anti-Semitism and imperialism. He claims that democracy, Christianity, and technology have provided the kind of historical context in which totalitarianism naturally developed. He asserts that democracy, with its freedom to organize politically, has provided fertile grounds upon which a single-party state could achieve or seize power. Also, "the fact that Christianity has tended to establish a broad predilection for convictional certainty" has given support to totalitarian ideologies. Finally, technological development tends toward greater size and influence of organization and methods, giving support to totalitarianism. On the last point, Friedrich says: "The citizen as an individual, and indeed in larger groups, is simply defenseless against the overwhelming technological superiority of those who can centralize in their hands the means wherewith to wield these modern arms and thereby physically to coerce." [9]

The number of preconditions increases. George F. Kennan, in describing what totalitarian Germany and Russia have in common, suggests five features: (1) both are great countries; (2) their totalitarianism came in the wake of a terribly costly and exhausting military effort, the First World War; (3) they have other highly significant similarities, such as the overthrow of a monarchy and a prelude of an unsuccessful liberal era; (4) both countries were influenced by the growth of secular national feeling, especially in the nineteenth century, and (5) both of these countries were great military land powers, characterized long before their respective revolutions by a high degree of centralization.[10]

Although other preconditions have been suggested to explain the *whys* of modern totalitarianism, it is evident from the listings above that no consensus has yet been reached on the subject. Criticisms may be raised, moreover, of almost every precondition that has been offered. Thus, Hannah Arendt's preconditions may be more applicable to Nazi Germany than to the Soviet Union. Anti-Semitism, moreover, can scarcely be offered as a universal precondition for all totalitarianism, and even for Nazi Germany, the picture was much more complex. Other factors come readily to mind. The 1920s were inhospitable to democracy and were congenial to authoritarian regimes. The German people had a well-known hostility to parliamentary institutions. The upper classes in imperial Germany were antidemocratic, and leading thinkers of that period boasted about their nation's differences from and superiority to other countries. These and other factors have been noted by German and other scholars.[11]

Similarly, the preconditions suggested by Friedrich are inadequate when applied, for example, to the Soviet Union. Obviously czarist Russia was far from being a democratized and technologized society. If anything, it was just the opposite. Russian orthodoxy, moreover, is commonly not thought to be characterized by "convictional certainty"; it is a highly mystical, nonintellectual, and credally immature form of Christianity. Thus, it is difficult to see what Friedrich's preconditions have to do with Soviet totalitarianism. In fact, it might be claimed that where the three preconditions exist in lively and developed forms, totalitarianism has not taken root.

The fact is that totalitarianism, by one definition or another, has occurred in various times and places. Leaving the definition of totalitarianism until the next section of this chapter, the following examples would need to be considered, among others, in any proper assessment: Communist China, the Soviet Union, National Socialist Germany, Fascist Italy, Franco's Spain, Salazar's Portugal, Peron's Argentina, Paraguay under the Jesuits, Poland under Pilsudski and his successors, Rumania under Carol II and Antonescu, Greece under Metaxas, ancient Rome, and ancient Egypt.

All of these cases of national states in which unlimited authority was expressed in one manner or another might be grist for the mill of totalitarian classification, yet each is historically unique. Every historical situation must be taken on its own, but the question arises of to what degree historically unique situations are comparable. For example, the totalitarian similarities between Nazi Germany and the Soviet Union appear to be so obvious and striking that many trained observers, as well as laymen everywhere, are prone to consider them two brush strokes out of a common pot of paint. Despite whatever similarities they may possess, however, as social forms they present a number of striking contrasts. Several may be noted. The Nazi leaders enjoyed a fairly high degree of mass support in their day, while communism was introduced by a small minority in the Soviet Union, and has been maintained the same way. Ideologically the two countries differ: Hitler's ideology had a very restricted appeal, especially to a national-racial constituency, while Lenin's ideology presumably appealed to the masses everywhere. Again, Marxism has purported to be a superscience, but National Socialism never claimed to have found a mode of thought which superseded all traditional intellectual labor. A final distinction is worth noting: Nazi Germany's totalitarianism, fortunately, did not live long enough to come to full bloom; but totalitarianism in the Soviet Union has had a number of decades in which to realize itself.

Totalitarianism is a product of the creative imagination as well as of concrete historicity. Some fictional works on the subject have illuminated the nature of the phenomenon. Thornton Wilder portrays Caesar as a totalitarian dictator in the making in *The Ides of March*. Similarly, the works of Kafka, Koestler, and the early Soviet satirists have illuminated the subject. The description of the future by George Orwell has fascinated a mass readership.[12]

NATURE

The question of the nature of totalitarianism is difficult to fathom. In general, however, two definitional possibilities exist. The first, the less adequate, defines totalitarianism in terms of one trait.[13] The difficulty is that investigators are not in agreement on the one definite trait necessary to establish the category of totalitarianism. The suggestions are manifold: a particularly designed economy, the acceptance of the dialectical theory of history, an assumption concerning class relations, a unique form of political organization, a set of ideas commonly called an ideology, a political stance toward culture (including education, the arts, religion, and science), an "imperialistic" vitality in international relations, the reliance upon terror and force in all human relations, and a phenomenon related to basic individual and social characteristics. Each of these suggestions has its own fervid advocates, and each is able to make some rational case for itself.

Even among those who hold to one definite trait, however, there is disagreement regarding the manner in which the trait should be interpreted. Thus, the psychoanalyst Erik H. Erikson thinks the development of totalitarianism in a particular society a socially definable growth almost identical with the development of the individual personality, including specific infantile and adolescent stages, mental disturbances, and particular "character structures."[14] On the other hand, Else Frankel-Brunswik, with a somewhat different psychological orientation, tends to interpret totalitarianism as a consequent mode of interpersonal adjustment of a particular personality type, the "authoritarian personality."[15] Similar disagreement exists among those who advocate other singular traits.

The alternative and more adequate way of defining totalitarianism is in terms of a configuration of traits. The basic assumption underlying the configurational interpretation of totalitarianism is the understanding that societies are essentially institutional systems rather than a hodge-podge of discrete traits. Totalitarian society, like any other society, consists of social relations and patterns that are of almost infinite complexity but are characterized by a discernible and definable form. Totalitarianism is a particular form of society. While it falls into the general classification of dictatorship, it is not the same as the ancient autocracies, tyrannies, despotisms, absolute monarchies, and traditional dictatorships. It is, in effect, a new form of dictatorship.[16]

The elements which basically compose the societal pattern of totalitarianism have been identified by Carl J. Friedrich as five. First, an official ideology which consists of an official body of doctrine covering all phases of the society's life and pointing in the direction of a perfect or final state of human affairs. Second, a single mass party, usually consisting of a small percentage of the total population, which is passionately dedicated to the realization of the ideology; a strict hierarchy, including a supreme leader, characterizes the party organization. Third, a monopolistic control, usually by the party, of all means of armed combat. Fourth, a similarly monopolistic control, in the same hands, of all means of mass communication. Fifth, the presence of a highly developed system of terroristic police control for the purpose of eliminating "enemies" of the society and enforcing orthodoxy upon the masses.[17] These five factors, then, in combination and interrelationship, characterize the modern totalitarian state and set it apart from other historically grounded forms of dictatorship. Friedrich's careful analysis has been captured in Brzezinski's definition: "Totalitarianism is a system in which technologically advanced instruments of political power are wielded without restraint by centralized leadership of an elite movement, for the purpose of effecting a total social revolution, including the conditioning of man, on the basis of certain arbitrary ideological assumptions proclaimed by the leadership, in an atmosphere of coerced unanimity of the entire population." [18]

Brzezinski, moreover, happily stresses, both in this definition and elsewhere, the dynamic or revolutionary character of totalitarianism. Totalitarianism is not an abstract and static social pattern; it is dynamic, always in a state of becoming. To some degree totalitarianism merely tolerates the burdens of the present form of society in order that its ideal projection of the society of the future may be achieved. Totalitarianism's dynamism may be placed in the intellectual context of a Hegelian interpretation of history or simply in terms of inevitable stages which are necessary to the realization of the "perfect" society. But, so far as the leadership of totalitarian societies is concerned, the dynamic aspects of the over-all social pattern commonly are considered to be institutionalized revolution.

Ideology

Whatever else totalitarianism may be, it is characterized by ideology. Ideology has been defined as "essentially an action program suitable for mass consumption, derived from certain doctrinal assumptions about the general nature of the dynamics of social reality, and combining some assertions about the inadequacies of the past and-or present with some explicit guides to action for improving the situation and some notions of the desired eventual state of affairs." [19] Thus, ideology is primarily a system of comprehensive belief which possesses practical implications for the guidance of individual and social life. In a sense, an ideology is a secular theology, in that it claims an ultimate comprehension of reality without a validly religious base. An ideology is a monistic system, that is, it formally advocates a single and uniform understanding of reality. Ideology also is all-inclusive. This means that no phase of individual life or society escapes its controlling influence. Similarly, ideology is exclusive, that is, it agressively denies the claims of all other theologies and ideologies. Moreover, it calls for a total commitment on the part of believers. Nothing less than total engagement is possible. Finally, an ideology is soteriological; it offers a plan of salvation, a means of escaping the real or imagined ills of the present.

The simple identification of ideology with totalitarianism has been questioned by some. Waldemar Gurian, for example, assumes that ideologies by themselves are not necessarily totalitarian. He claims that totalitarian ideologies should be called "ideocracies," since totalitarianism changes ordinary ideologies into ideas intended for the institutionalization of revolution.[20] On the other hand, Hannah Arendt claims that totalitarian ideology is categorized by being strictly the logic of an idea, a logical process developed from a single idea. Thus, she advocates the substitution of "logocracy" for ideology.[21]

It is true, of course, that totalitarian ideology is not held on a take-it-or-leave-it basis, but constitutes an appealing and compelling mystique of belief that separates it from other, more mundane ideologies. In fact, totalitarian ideology possesses a religious character in the intensity of the emotional fervor with which it is offered and accepted. In this spirit, then, H. G. Wood, for example, terms communism the "Fundamentalism of the Socialist Movement." [22] In fact, totalitarian and other ideologies have at times been likened to theologies, and the resulting bodies of believers, to social institutions similar to and competitive with the churches. Lewis S. Feuer states:

Marxism has often been described as a religion; it can be called the first secular world religion. Its dialectic is akin to Calvinist predestination; like other creeds, it has its sacred text, its saints, its heretics, its elect, its holy city. If Marx was its Messiah, Lenin was its St. Paul. But after all these analogies have been made, what remains to be emphasized is how different Marxism is from other religions. Unlike Christianity, for instance, its appeal has always been first to the intellectuals. Christianity was resisted by the ancient philosophers, who regarded it as an aberration of the lower classes; it spread from below upwards. Marxism, on the contrary, has been carried by the intellectuals to the proletarians and peasants.[23]

Surely the ideological pretensions of totalitarian regimes puts them in contrast, competition, and conflict not only with the churches but with all other independent and "free" elements in society. A demonstrably clear source of antagonism between church and state in a totalitarian society lies at the point of ideology.

Politics

Totalitarianism is characterized by a distinctive politics; it is total politics. It is a form of society in which all elements of the social order are under the control of a highly centralized political leadership. This leadership is centered primarily in a party organization of utterly devoted disciples and leaders. The party commonly is bureaucratically organized, with clear, hierarchical statuses and authorities. At the top a charismatic leader ("the cult of personality") stands supreme over all. In the life of the solitary leader presumably are embodied all of the finest virtues of the party, and indeed of the mass followership. This all-powerful, superhuman leader glows with strength, superiority, and glory, and affords all others, within the party and without, a sense of protection, defense, and security.

Just as totalitarianism is characterized by an in-group of political elites, the party, it is also characterized by some out-group which is rejected *in toto*. The out-group often becomes the scapegoat of the elites, a real or imagined enemy for whose defeat the loyalties and energies of the whole society are called.

Totalitarianism is politically characterized by distinctive attitudes toward political parties, the judiciary, and the legislature. A totalitarian in-group cannot tolerate political nonconformity. Thus, it cannot tolerate more than one political party. The pressure of a conformist ideology and the realities of anxious elitist control bring party leaders to the assumption that political nonconformity is essentially treason. As Jerzy G. Gliksman states for the Soviet Union: ". . . there is no place for legal political opposition and therefore no other possible logical outlet for divergent political opinions but 'counterrevolutionary' acts." [24]

Another political characteristic of totalitarian regimes is the subversion of the independence of the judiciary. An independent judiciary is commonly based upon the assumption that laws and their application enjoy an autonomous existence to which even political leaders ought to be bound. But in totalitarianism the political leaders are the ideologues, those who are charged with the formulation of orthodoxy and its application to all spheres of the society. So in totalitarianism the judiciary cannot be tolerated as an independent body, but must be viewed by the political leadership as simply another institution to which a politically determined orthodoxy properly should be applied. Totalitarianism also cannot tolerate a genuinely independent legislature. It is true that totalitarian societies, such as Fascist Italy, National Socialist Germany, the Soviet Union, and Communist China, regularly have general and special elections under the terms of their constitutions, but the resulting machinery of government can scarcely be called independent. Commonly, in the light of the absence of more than one political party, the candidates are hand-picked by the governing elite. Also, the resulting legislatures are not known to enjoy a genuinely autonomous existence. Despite constitutions and elections and other attributes of political procedure, totalitarian political leadership concentrates full and final power in itself. For the Soviet Union, for example, Brzezinski states that "underneath fictitious lip service to federalism and the importance of local initiative, central executive control is indisputable and has been so during the entire Soviet period. . . ." [25]

Totalitarianism, then, is a form of society in which the various features of political organization are under the strict and total control of the politically elite, the final managers of political power in a totalitarian society. But additional features of society come under strict political control under totalitarianism. Science, for example, cannot exist even as an independent but sympathetic body of knowledge and practice. Under totalitarianism science in all its aspects is, like law, an aspect of society to which the political elites apply the appropriate elements of the all-encompassing ideology. The question, for example, is not whether Lysenko is objectively correct or not, but whether Lysenko's views are consonant with the over-all ideology of the Soviet Union. This perversion of the objective claims of science to the partisan uses of totalitarianism has been lamented by many, including H. J. Muller:

The politicians of the Iron Curtain countries, in their blighting attacks on several important branches of science, and especially in their complete destruction of genetics, have provided an amazing object lesson of the disaster which can befall science even in our time when one small group of men, arrogating to themselves all power, become convinced of the superiority of their judgments in all directions and, with the aid of modern physical and social techniques, succeed in subjecting all human activities, including science, to their own dictation.[26]

What happens under totalitarianism to science is what happens to all other aspects of society. All of the associations, social institutions, interpretations of the past, expressions of art, education of the young and the professionals, the activities of the intelligentsia, all inevitably and completely come under the sway of the political elite. This is the core meaning of totalitarianism. It means that the total life of a society is managed by a centrally directing minority who accept and serve an institutionally revolutionary ideology.

Even the individual is controlled. The rights of individuals have had a long history. Even in European countries in the past centuries inequality was both a social and legal fact, but by the end of the nineteenth century practically all civilized countries had established the legal or formal equality of all men. Constitutional safeguards protecting the rights of the individual against the state widely came to be a fact of social life. In this period, as Hans Kohn points out, "arbitrariness by the powerful or by the police and censorship of beliefs or opinions seemed to belong to a dead past." [27]

TOTALITARIANISM AND THE CHURCHES

Implicit in this chapter are a number of assumptions that might make it appear that the churches are the inveterate and unconditional opponents of totalitarian states. Some of the grounds of opposition will shortly be examined in some detail, but it is well, in the interests of objectivity, to admit readily that totalitarianism and the churches have not always been mortal enemies. Two types of affinity may be noted. First, authoritarian churches working closely with autocratic governments on occasion have provided the effective preconditioning for the rise of totalitarianism. John Gunther, for example, has pointed to the fact that for centuries the unity of the Orthodox Church and of the czarist regimes dominated Russia in such a way that the national culture was deeply influenced and the nation was made receptive to the rise of totalitarianism.[28] Similarly, the culturally forming influence of the Roman Catholic Church is probably not without relationship to the rise of Franco's Falangism in Spain.[29]

Second, the churches on occasion have accommodated themselves to totalitarian government, giving some measure of support in return for some measure of recognition and protection. A fine example of such accommodation involves the Orthodox Church and the government of the Soviet Union. The process has been described in some detail by Matthew Spinka.[30] Spinka, for example, describes the sharp and dramatic change in the policy positions of Patriarch Sergei within a span of about one year. On June 10, 1926, he issued a statement which called upon the Soviet leadership to recognize the Orthodox Church as the "registered" or legally recognized religious body for the nation. The patriarch, while promising civil loyalty, refrained from fulsome phrases of support for the government and, in fact, expressed considerable reserve regarding church responsibility for anti-Soviet political activity. Sergei was arrested and remained in prison for three and a half months. On July 29, 1927, he issued the Declaration of 1927, which showed that his position clearly had changed from that of "strict separation of the ecclesiastical and the political spheres of activity to one of complete co-operation with, and submission to, the government." [31] The cooperative relationships between the Orthodox Church and the Soviet government since that time are well known. Similar accommodations by the churches to totalitarian regimes are a sad but familiar feature of recent international history.

Competition of Absolutes

Totalitarianism, as explained earlier, rests fundamentally upon absolutist assumptions. Totalitarian ideology claims to possess the final, comprehensive, and inclusive understanding of reality. Totalitarian ideology can permit no serious competitors. Also, totalitarian states employ politics, especially through the use of domination and terroristic methods, to enforce the total claim of their ideologies upon every aspect of individual and social living. Since totalitarian governments claim supremacy over the whole of life, they cannot tolerate free, independent, and autonomous centers of social organization. The churches, as has been shown, are not the only social institutions which may come into conflict with totalitarian states. All of the social institutions, to the degree that they understand their independent validity and are characterized by some degree of social vitality, are prone to resist the encroachment of totalitarian governments. But the churches at their best possess a clearly transcendental vision of themselves and, indeed, of life itself. Thus, the churches constitute a foremost social institution of resistance to the totalitarian claims of government. Vital churches have resisted the substitution of any ultimate for God. This competition of absolutes accounts in part for the conflict between church and state in National Socialist Germany, for as Max Ascoli and Arthur Feiler state: "For National Socialism the Nation was God from the beginning." [32] No wonder, then, that the German churches were a major source of resistance to the totalitarian claims of Hitler.

In this connection, the thesis of Franklin H. Littell bears respect. He argues that the capacity of religious bodies to resist totalitarianism lies in the "role of dogmatic formulas in laying grounds for and developing a disciplined community of opposition." Littell examines church experience during the National Socialist era in Germany. He points out that the overliberal and secularized versions of Christianity in that period, then called "positive Christianity," were by and large amenable to an accommodation with Hitlerism. The clearly resisting elements within the German churches, however, took their stand on grounds that were "narrowly churchly and theological rather than general and humane." As an example of this resistance, Littell notes the comprehensive statement of thirteen articles, entitled "What We Believe, and What We Do not Believe," which was drawn up and circulated against the ideology of the German Army of Occupation and its Dutch adherents by the resisting church in the Netherlands. One article makes clear the absolute claim of the church over the absolute claim of the state:

Moreover, we do *not* believe that the sovereignty of our rightful Lord extends only over our souls, so that some other domination be it State, Nation, leader, can claim unlimited dominion over our bodies. Obedience to our Savior, Jesus Christ, takes precedence over every other obedience, even before every other lawful obedience, such as parents and civic authorities.

This view, when clearly held by the churches, enabled them to be effective resisters of totalitarianism as political religion. As Littell concludes: "And it is in the thrust 'to make everything alike' that the totalitarian state has run afoul of the universalism of the Christian churches, and will continue to do so whenever there are faithful men to stand up and be counted for the sake of the Lord of History." [33]

Reversion to Primitivism

Totalitarian ideologies seek to enlist men's energies in the obtaining of a "perfect" society of the future. Paradoxically, however, this future is based upon a reversion to

primitivism. Totalitarianism does not call man to more
inclusive and universal loyalties, but to partial and sectarian devotion to race or class. Totalitarianism calls man
to a future which is not the logical development of history, but a clear and traumatic break with historical development. For the achievement of history's support of
totalitarianism, totalitarian leaders regularly are required
to distort history, making it serve their own purposes.

Totalitarianism, moreover, merely appears to be rational. In reality, it is sustained by the reign of terror, both
in control of its citizenry and as a threat to the external
world. For these and other reasons, totalitarianism constitutes a threat to historical development as well as to
humane values.

Two of these points may be illustrated. Racism, in the
light of history, constitutes man's ancient curse and
present shame. Yet the future, one hopes, will see the
diminution of existing racial conditions and hatreds. It
is in this spirit that President Lyndon B. Johnson invoked
the spirit of Abraham Lincoln to condemn racial suspi-
cions, racial hatred, and racial violence in a major address
on Lincoln's Birthday in February 1967.[34] As Hannah
Arendt, for example, has shown for National Socialism,
racism is a fundamental part of the totalitarian philosophy. It calls man not to the future but to the past. On this
score Arendt states:

Racism may indeed carry out the doom of the Western World
and, for that matter, of the whole of human civilization. . . .
For no matter what learned scientists may say, race is, politically speaking, not the beginning of humanity, but its end, not
the origin of peoples but their decay, not the natural birth of
man but his unnatural death.[35]

Totalitarianism also does not constitute the fulfillment of human history and society. It destroys society, repudiating society as it has developed over the long centuries. No less an authority than Winston Churchill has perceived this aspect of totalitarianism in his analysis of the Soviet Union under Lenin:

Lenin was the Grand Repudiator. He repudiated everything. He repudiated God, King, Country, morals, treaties, death, rents, interest, the laws and customs of centuries, all contracts written or implied, the whole structure—such as it is of human society. In the end he repudiated himself. He repudiated the communist system.

When death seized him, "the Russian people were left floundering in the bog. Their worst misfortune was his birth; their next worst—his death." [36]

Preventing Totalitarianism

Totalitarianism, like other social formations, is never static. As a dynamic social process and form, it is adaptable. Thus, Carmen Irizarry describes the manner in which contemporary Spain is undergoing deep unrest, active dissent, and pressures for change, especially in church-state relations.[37] The Soviet Union also is undergoing vast and significant changes.[38] So, too, the relations of church and state in Latin America are far from harmonious. In fact, as Frederick B. Pike has demonstrated, the relations between church and state in Latin America have been quite different from those assumed in the popular mind.[39] What the future will hold for totalitarianism in general and for the relations between the churches and totalitarian states in particular cannot be predicted with any degree of accuracy.

In summarizing how the nontotalitarian countries may resist totalitarianism in the future, Karl W. Deutsch says: "Our best defense during the next thirty years may well consist in the strengthening of the free world from the ground up and from the inside out, through the growth and strengthening of centers and core areas of genuine freedom." [40] The strengthening of the free world will, of course, require the strengthening of centers of pluralism and diversity within the national communities of the free nations. One of these centers obviously is the church. The growth of the church as a free center in a free society, not cursed with the ambition of dominating the state, socially minded and responsive, prophetic in its proclamations and grounded in a deep sense of history, is a social necessity.[41]

9

The Church and the Welfare State

THE STATE AND ECONOMICS

The key terms of "church" and "state" are usually kept quite vague in popular discussions of the relations of church and state. Thus, among some the "church" connotes an ethereal but positive entity, while the "state" is the representation of a necessary and coercive evil that may through proper handling be of some benefit, especially to partisan groups. Chapter 2 sought to show the complexities that are involved in the use of the term "church," and Chapter 3 tried to provide a background for a more authentic understanding of the "state." In Chapter 3 it was claimed that two chief ideas have dominated the Western understanding of the state. The first claims an absolute legitimacy and autonomy for the state. The second asserts the liberal or empirical conception of the nature and function of the state. The second conception of the state has become generally prevalent among the Western nations and elsewhere and commonly is termed "the welfare state."

Although the welfare state is primarily concerned with the economic welfare of the citizenry, it also by being so creates proper questions for the relations of church and state, since historically the church has expressed deep concern regarding the welfare of the people. Also, the fact that the state as the welfare state in recent times conceives of itself as a benevolent power that is guided by the people themselves creates other questions regarding the relations of church and state. From this perspective, then, a review of the nature of the welfare state and its implications seems here to be appropriate.

HEILBRONER'S THREE TYPES

Robert L. Heilbroner has indicated that there are only three overarching types or systems by which societies have sought to solve their economic challenges. These great systemic types are categorized according to key characteristics: (1) tradition, (2) command, and (3) the market.[1]

Tradition

He claims that the first is the oldest and until a few years ago by far the most prevalent way of managing the economy. Tradition has its own answer to the problems of production and distribution. Sons are assigned to the jobs of their fathers in order that the needful tasks of the society be continued over the generations. Custom provides the basis upon which the old society faces new problems. The traditionally oriented economy tends to be a relatively static one. It tends to alleviate economic problems at the cost of economic progress.

Command

The method of command is also in a sense traditional; at least it has existed for a long time. This method features imposed authority. It may possess many of the characteristics of the traditional system, but the nature of its organization is radically different. The command method seeks to organize the economy in terms of a hierarchical system of power centers. At the top of the system is a person or group who acts as a commander-in-chief. The Egyptian Pharaoh Cheops employed the command method in the building of the pyramids, temples, and roads of ancient Egypt, but a different form of the same method is observable today in modern China and Russia, and in fact is evident also in democratic societies in times of crisis. The command system, however, favors neither tradition nor innovation; its dynamic rests ultimately upon the legitimacy of authority.

The Market

The third solution to the economic problem is the market organization of society. This method seeks to solve the problems of production and distribution with a minimum of reliance upon either tradition or command. Under this system the assumption is made that the free operations of economic institutions will tend to create their own harmony and result in the greater satisfaction of the material wants of the largest number of people. The market system is a constant source of wonderment, for by it the most complicated economic arrangements are maintained without the exclusively heavy hand of tradition or the dominance of a commanding power.

Heilbroner's classification of economic systems as characterized by tradition, command, and the market, describes "ideal types" as Max Weber spoke of theoretical constructs which nowhere exist in fact.[2] Heilbroner's theoretical constructs must be taken or considered in just such a way. They are constructs that create considerable insight regarding actual economic systems, but their very purity of exclusion limits their usefulness in economic discourse.

HEILBRONER'S TYPOLOGY
AND THE WELFARE STATE

The limitations of Heilbroner's typology are apparent when his threefold system is applied to such a phenomenon as the welfare state. The welfare state, to a degree, fits each of the three. It is a system which by now is traditional. It has made its way in many countries and has found wide acceptance. The term to be applied to the reality of the welfare state may be in dispute, and knowing people may debate one aspect or another of the general program of the welfare state. But in general the idea of the welfare state is an economic and political inheritance. That it is not a lively option economically or politically in several major nations is made clear by the fact that opposing political parties may differ as to the desirable extent of the welfare state, but seldom do they differ on the basic fact of its presence and worth.

The welfare state to some extent is a system of command. The welfare state is not bound by classical notions of laissez faire. There is room, sometimes ample room, within it for centralized governmental initiative and control. Nations that currently consider themselves to be welfare states also maintain some forms of general planning. The political leadership, moreover, may take command actions in specific instances, such as those involving inflation. The welfare state is based both on tradition and command.

The welfare state also rests to a degree upon the market organization of society. Most, if not all, of the current welfare states allow for some form of private ownership and initiative. Some welfare states seem to favor a parallelism between the public and private sectors of the economy, depending upon the full development of each to achieve the general welfare. To the extent to which they recognize the importance of the market as a self-regulating system in economics they are following Heilbroner's third method by which societies meet their economic challenges.

The main problem facing modern societies is not that of classifying systems of economics and politics. The welfare state represents a relatively recent development in history. It represents an effort to solve an age-long dilemma. This problem has been particularly evident and pressing to those who have cherished democratic values. The dilemma has grown from the contradictions inherent in the development within the last hundred years between political freedom and economic dependence.

Political freedom has been widely established in democratic nations. It is founded on the assumption that the holders of political power are ultimately accountable to the citizenry. It views the rulers of a nation as agents for the electorate. Political office is a trust in which the interests of the people are to be both protected and expressed.

Economically, however, the system of political democracy that has been established in many nations has never been achieved in the economic realm. There, the dominance of the market economy negates economic aspirations. Despite the importance of the labor movement, the major pattern of industrial organization is hierarchical with great power concentrated in the top range of the system. The corporation is run on discipline and obedience, not on a system of free elections in which actual power is held by those at the bottom of the hierarchical scale. The welfare state is a form of economics and politics by which benefits desired by the masses and not provided for by the industrial establishment are made possible through political means.

THE BEVERIDGE REPORT

Quite possibly the most important document in the last twenty years which has sought to solve the dilemma between political freedom and economic dependence is the so-called Beveridge Report.[3] This report is all the more remarkable since it was a government publication. Also, its importance was enhanced by the fact that it became, surprisingly enough, a best-seller in Britain and elsewhere. The Beveridge Report was further developed two years later in another significant document by Lord Beveridge.[4] Both documents represent a blueprint for Britain's welfare state. In addition to the delineation of specific ways in which the welfare state for Britain could be initiated, developed, and administered, the report deeply explored subjects of general, economic, and political concern.

Full Employment

One of the problems of the modern economy with which Beveridge was concerned is full employment. He was well aware of the difficulties in defining "full employment." Yet he stated that full employment within the aim of his report "means more vacant jobs than unemployed men." The purpose of employment is not merely to provide men with a source of income. Men, according to Beveridge, must have the chance of rendering useful service and a feeling that they are doing so. Employment similarly is a means to more consumption and more leisure; it signifies a higher standard of life. Employment in this sense cannot be equated with time-spending or time-wasting. Employment must be productive and progressive.

Beveridge recognizes that in an authoritarian society, the problem of full employment may be easily met. In a command economy everyone can readily be put to work, but Beveridge was exploring "methods of achieving full employment in a free society." He was concerned that all of the essential citizen liberties be preserved. He described these liberties as "freedom of worship, speech, writing, study and teaching; freedom of assembly and of association for political and other purposes, including the bringing about of a peaceful change of the governing authority; freedom in choice of occupation; and freedom in the management of a personal income." [5] Each of these freedoms he defines and describes at some length.

Private Property

Beveridge recognized the right to private property, but he questioned the significance of the private ownership of the means of production as an inalienable aspect of the British economy. He thought it may be a good economic device, but that it is not an essential citizen liberty in Britain because "it is not and never has been enjoyed by more than a very small proportion of the British people." But Beveridge's questioning of the private ownership of the means of production does not lead him to think that private enterprise is an evil. In fact, Beveridge holds firmly to private enterprise. Full employment, however, is a more primary requirement of society, and it cannot be won and held without "a great extension of the responsibilities and powers of the state exercised through organs of the central Government." On this tenet, much of the case of the welfare state depends. Beveridge thought that no power less than that of the state is able to ensure adequate total outlay. At all times the central government must take control in the general interest in the location of industry and in the use of the land. One cannot ask for full employment, he wrote, and at the same time resist the extension of governmental activity. Such a course, to him, is like "shouting for victory in total war while rejecting compulsory service and rationing."

Democratic Government

Yet the policy for full employment and its implementation in the welfare state, in Beveridge's view, is to be carried out democratically by public authorities, central and local. Authorities are responsible ultimately to the voters. Thus, the welfare state as envisioned by Beveridge would maintain all the essential liberties, which are "more precious than full employment itself." Beveridge believed, moreover, that the welfare state, far from restricting liberties, was a social device by which personal liberties would be given their necessary support and fuller extension.

In his advocacy of the welfare state, Beveridge steered clear of speaking favorably of socialism. When he considered the general issue of public ownership as against private enterprise, he reached the "provisional conclusion" that the need for socialism "has not yet been demonstrated." In practically all matters, however, Beveridge was an empiricist. He was willing to make decisions for or against particular economic and political arrangements; he shunned the advocacy of broad and doctrinaire systems of organization. He claimed that the basic proposals of his report "will work under capitalism and under socialism alike."

Social and Health Services

The empirical or pragmatic approach by Beveridge to the requirements of full employment led him not only to accept the extension of central government control in economic matters; it also brought him to the conclusion that the stresses and strains of a reordered and developing economy necessarily create temporary and even permanent problems for the citizenry. Thus, the economy of the welfare state can never fully eliminate unemployment. The economy and the state should make it possible for those who lose their jobs to find new jobs at fair wages within their capacity and without delay, but the satisfaction of this demand assumes some measure of unemployment which is basic to the problems of economic adjustment. Therefore, Beveridge advocated a governmentally maintained system of unemployment insurance. Such a system insures some income to the unemployed person (and his family) and alleviates material want and feelings of personal insecurity.

Beveridge also was able to recognize the existence and influence of continuing problems for individuals and their families beyond that of unemployment. For example, a state must recognize that a small number of its citizens will be incapacitated for one reason or another from accepting full employment even when it is available. These may suffer from chronic illnesses, physical deformities or lacks, mental disabilities, old age, and similar limitations. Beveridge concluded that the humane or welfare state could not rely ultimately upon that form of private enterprise which is philanthropy or charity to meet the relatively large and significant problems of this group of limited citizens. The state, he wrote, has a basic and full responsibility for their welfare. On the basis of this assumption, he advocated the extension of governmental, social, and medical services.

The social and medical services were not conceived by Beveridge as the cardinal requirements of the welfare state; full employment was that. Rather, they were social necessities easily justified by a rising standard of living resulting from full employment. Beveridge rested his case for social and health services not upon abstract Christian principles, but upon the requirements of an efficient economic system and the responsibilities of the state for the well-being of all its citizens. He appealed less to lofty motivations on the part of self-giving individuals than he did upon the power of the central government to provide benefits to a limited group of its citizenry through compulsory taxation.

Although the actual course of the development of the welfare state in Britain did not follow precisely the recommendations of Beveridge and his followers, nevertheless, his studies and writings are testimony themselves to the power of human thought to influence the course of nations.

PRINCIPLES OF
THE WELFARE STATE

On the basis of Beveridge's report and other statements on the nature of the welfare state, a number of basic principles may be deduced as fundamentally characterizing this widely prevalent form of economic and political development in modern times. Obviously, the principles overlap.

Material Well-Being

First, every individual, despite his circumstances, is entitled to a minimum of material well-being. The definition of "minimum" may be debated, but it generally includes such matters as food, clothing, and housing. In some instances, health services, vocational counseling and rehabilitation, and types or degrees of education may be considered within the minimum. The assumption underlying this principle, however, is the dignity and worth of every human being. The assumption infers that every person has a basic social right to life and at least some forms of the pursuit of happiness. Insofar as the private sector of the economy is able to satisfy the person's individual wants and aspirations, it should be permitted to do so. Also insofar as private enterprise in philanthropy or charity is able to meet pressing human wants, it should be permitted and encouraged to make its contribution.

Expanding Living Standards

Second, expanding living standards are a result of an expanding economic system. The social benefits of the welfare state are not conceived as being dependent upon a static economy. The welfare state does not base its welfare economics on the assumption that those who presently possess economic advantages must necessarily be denied these advantages. As full employment becomes a reality, the productive capacity of the economy increases. The benefits to the people are financed in large part out of the increases. They are financed in large part out of the gains achieved and enjoyed by the entire national community.

At least three elements are basic to the maintenance of an expanding economy. First, there must be the fullest utilization of natural resources. These constitute an indispensable base upon which agricultural and industrial development can take place. Second, the utilization of scientific knowledge is required. While natural resources constitute a natural limitation upon the full development of an economy, they are far more flexible and malleable than commonly conceived. But there is virtually no limit to the development of scientific knowledge. Such knowledge is a purely human affair. By it, limited natural resources can be made to grant benefits to consumers that otherwise would be impossible. Thus, sand may be sand, but through the application of scientific knowledge it may be transformed into a variety of products enjoyed by consumers. Third, an expanding economy also depends upon the proper utilization of human manpower. Such an economy cannot rely wholly upon the market organization of society. Some degree of central governmental control and direction is desirable. The problem of unemployment, for example, cannot be viewed simply as a natural consequence of the workings of a market economy. The state, by controls and planning, is able to direct and redirect the efficient utilization of human manpower.

The expansion of living standards, furthermore, within the conception of the welfare state does not necessarily rest upon exclusively material standards. The welfare state defines "expanding living standards" as encompassing a wide range of nonmaterial benefits.

The General Welfare

Third, the state has a right to exercise its "general welfare" responsibility. The welfare state does not view the fundamental functions of government in negative terms. It presupposes that the state has a positive responsibility to contribute to the general welfare of the citizenry. The extent to which the state exercises its responsibility may depend upon a variety of factors. It may or may not intrude into essentially private spheres, according to the democratically defined and developed philosophy of its responsibility, but generally the welfare state assumes that it possesses the responsibility to act in those instances when private initiative has failed to solve a pressing problem or when the results of private initiative are judged to be deleterious to the general welfare.

Empiricism

Fourth, each economic and political issue is judged on its own merits. The welfare state is decidedly empiricist in its philosophy and actions. It avoids dogmatic solutions such as those that can readily be labeled "capitalist" or "socialist." It draws its strength from its flexibility in meeting problems as they occur and devising solutions appropriate to particular problems. Such a state is not characterized by the purity of its economic and political abstractions. It rests, as with the common-law tradition of the English-speaking peoples, upon an empiricism and experimentalism that are congenial to the psychological and institutional framework of a democratic society.

HISTORIC ASPECTS OF THE WELFARE STATE

The welfare state did not develop full-blown overnight in democratic societies. It followed a gradualist approach to the changing economic and social factors of modern living. In the United States, for example, the idea of the welfare state has been growing into reality for decades. It is possible to trace this development from Theodore Roosevelt's "Square Deal" through Woodrow Wilson's "New Freedom" to Franklin Roosevelt's "New Deal" and beyond. Such growth, moreover, cannot be discussed accurately in terms of inevitability. Almost nothing in the democratic tradition is inevitable. The empirical basis for the welfare state's activities is economic matters and in providing social and health benefits to the people leads to the giving up of some old solutions (for example, relief in kind) and to the resistance to new measures federally sponsored (for example, medical care for the aged).

A careful reading of history demonstrates that the welfare state is not the radical innovation that some consider it to be. Everyone who has believed in the necessity for some form of the state has assigned it functions. The laissez-faire economist Adam Smith believed that the state's functions included justice, defense, education, and roads and communications.[6] Other economists have granted the state even more responsibilities. They have said that the state has a duty in respect to those things which only the state can enforce, such as justice and defense. To these duties have been added those which diffuse benefits for which the beneficiaries cannot be charged, such as lighthouses. A third category of governmental responsibility includes those things in which the judgment of the state is supposed to be superior to that of the citizens, such as for how many years children should be schooled. Some citizens sincerely believe that the state too freely exercises its responsibilities in the last category, while others, like John Kenneth Galbraith, believe that the state, even the modern welfare state, has not been active enough in determining the ends to which natural and human resources should be put.[7] But the final determiner of the extent to which a state should assume responsibilities for the citizenry in a political democracy is ultimately the electorate which responds to party platforms and political personalities at the times of election.

Planning

If planning may be taken as a primary aspect of the welfare state, then it may be said that the United States has had a welfare state from its very inception. The Constitutional Convention itself is an example of economic and political planning on a grand scale, for the Constitution not only created a democratic system of government but also enunciated special plans on currency, tariffs, interstate commerce, and international relations. Alexander Hamilton (1757-1804), in his 1791 "Report on Manufactures," sought to establish a national policy in regard to industry and fields of American interest related to it. Albert Gallatin (1761-1849) drew up a plan of ways in which to improve the fiscal situation of the United States in his capacity as Secretary of the Treasury under Jefferson. Henry Clay (1777-1852), in 1820, sponsored an "American System" in which tariffs and internal improvements were prominently considered. Also, the American Homestead Policy of 1862 was designated to provide a homestead at a nominal cost to almost anyone who sought a place on the land. These plans and actions of long ago are merely representative of many more that have occurred in the national life from its inception until now. American tradition, therefore, has not shunned planning and action for the general welfare by the federal government. From this perspective, the welfare state in the United States is not a recent innovation; it is characteristic of much of the entire development of the country.

EVALUATION OF THE WELFARE STATE

The previous discussion of the nature of the welfare state is admittedly sketchy and incomplete. Obviously, many qualifications will need to be made of the materials presented. Clearly, also, there are those who will disagree with one aspect or another of it or even with the whole presentation. Despite these shortcomings, however, it is desirable that the welfare state be evaluated. Thus, certain negative and positive tendencies inherent in the idea of the welfare state will be examined briefly.

Negative Tendencies

It may well be that those who are critical of the welfare state derive their views from an essentially pessimistic philosophy of human nature and of the state. Such a fundamental attitude toward man and society probably undergirds any particular criticism of the welfare state in conscious and systematic form. Thus, such social systems as democracy, anarchy, and socialism are essentially based upon optimistic estimates of man and society. They affirm the possibility of the reformation of man, that progress is possible, and that human reason can be trusted in social decision making.

The political pessimist, on the other hand, at times denies that man is capable of progressive improvement, that the very idea of progress is substantial, and that human reason is a vital and normative principle in social affairs. Traditionally, the optimistic view has been characterized as sentimental or utopian, while the pessimistic outlook has carried the banner of "realism." Actually, however, neither *a priori* assumption is persuasive. The critical intelligence should not permit the attachment of such labels to broad-scale philosophies without patient and extensive recourse to evidence.

Those who hold an essentially pessimistic view of man and society have appeared in almost every generation. Some have created systems of thought that bear careful attention. Niccolò Machiavelli (1469-1527), who published *The Prince* in 1513, was such a thinker. Machiavelli, among other things, clearly differentiated between political means and techniques and political ideals and aims. Many persons before him and afterward have looked upon the employment of political power as a means for the attainment of higher ends. Such ends classically have been considered to be man's individual and social freedom, the attainment of fundamentally religious values, and the maintenance and development of justice itself.

Machiavelli stood opposed to that tradition. He looked upon political power as an end to be sought and maintained in itself. In other words, he radically separated ethics from politics, making politics amoral. The separation of ethics from politics is evident in Machiavelli's statement:

For how we live is so far removed from how we ought to live that he who abandons what is done for what ought to be done, will rather learn to bring about his own ruin than his preservation. A man who wishes to make a profession of goodness in everything must necessarily come to grief among so many who are not good. Therefore, it is necessary for a prince, who wishes to maintain himself, to learn how not to be good, and to use this knowledge and not use it, according to the necessity of the case.[8]

Machiavelli believed that the seizure and effective maintenance of power depends upon two basic principles: law and force. Man, he admitted, prefers the former; the beasts exemplify the latter, but both methods need to be used by the seeker and holder of political power. The prince must "know well how to use both the beast and the man." From Machiavelli's observations, all power organizations depend upon "methods." He noted that the leaders of the churches operated in the defense of their power in the same unholy and ruthless manner as did the political rulers of nations.

Thus, he concluded that every power center is corrupt —the state no less than any other. Machiavelli, furthermore, was not dogmatically for or against any particular political system. In the *Discourses,* published in 1521, he discussed republicanism favorably.[9] Although his generally pessimistic view of the political order may be assumed to be antidemocratic, there is reason to think that Machia-

velli believed that he was describing the universal situation so far as the deployment of political power is concerned.

Other political philosophers, while differing among
themselves, also have pessimistic estimates of the state.
Thomas Hobbes (1588-1679) taught that the state of nature is a continual war or threat of war of every man
against every other man. Hobbes, the son of an English
clergyman, taught that man is in "continual fear and
danger of violent death" and that the life of man is "solitary, poor, nasty, brutish, and short." [10] Like Hobbes,
John Locke (1632-1704) believed in the state of nature,
but had a different interpretation of it. He advocated a
strongly organized central government, the sovereign state,
so strong and powerful that it readily could withstand
its enemies from within or without. He opposed any principle, such as division of power, mixed government,
liberty of the subject, the right of the individual to question the legality of the sovereign's actions, that would
weaken the autonomy of the state. Absolute obedience on
the part of the citizen to the state is required in Locke's
view.

While Machiavelli, Hobbes, and Locke differed on
many important matters, they were united in maintaining
an essentially pessimistic view of the state. All of them
deeply questioned the rational and ethical character of
man in his social conduct. All laid a basis for a skeptical
attitude toward power and its uses. Therefore, they laid
an articulate and profound basis for modern criticism of
the welfare state. No state, no matter how benign its
avowed purposes might be, should be trusted. The pur-

pose of government in their view is not to enhance the
welfare of the citizenry, but to maintain social order by
whatever methods are required.

In modern times, a number of critics of the welfare
state have arisen. The late Joseph A. Schumpeter, for example, directly questioned the efficacy of the full-employ-
ment economics advocated by William Beveridge.[11] Schumpeter thinks that Beveridge's notions are more suited to a
period in which large-scale unemployment is a vexing
problem. He shows that full employment is not necessarily
a solution to the problems that the welfare state seeks to
solve. For example, full employment may merely aggra-
vate rather than alleviate the problem of the bureau-
cratization of business organizations. Bureaucracy in society is a problem which the welfare state tends to accen-
tuate rather than eliminate.

Other critics of the welfare state have claimed that social
planning by government, a chief feature of the welfare
state, is a necessary prelude to the development of dictatorship. Walter Lippmann, for example, was among the first
to raise this criticism.[12] Similarly Friedrich A. Hayek, in
a widely read book, advanced the same thesis, utilizing a
questionable analogy whereby he sought to show that socialism was the backdrop in Germany for the development
of Nazi totalitarianism; therefore, he claimed, similar
trends in England and the United States would culminate
in a similar result.

Some elements within middle-class Protestantism in
the United States and elsewhere also have been opposed
to the welfare state on a variety of grounds. In part, these
critics have been fearful of the encroachments of government upon the free exercise of religion. Also, they have

been persuaded of the desirability of a voluntaristic economy in which individualism is supreme as an ideological parallel to the individualism in religion (which some strands of traditional Protestantism have initiated and nourished). In addition, some Protestants as well as others have tended to view the welfare state as a threat to the historical responsibilities of the churches for providing welfare and other benefits to those who are in need of them. Thus, some sectors within Protestantism even today are strongly critical of the welfare state.

Positive Tendencies

The idea of the welfare state is controversial. Some strongly oppose it, while others defend it as the best possible economic and political system. The articulate criticisms and defense of the system, however, are mainly found among those who have a specialized interest and even competency in dealing with the idea in detail. Whether the idea is a good one or not, it is evident that the great masses of people in our time, expressing themselves regularly through popular and free elections, have voted in favor of the welfare state. The degree of the support of the people varies from nation to nation as does the resulting nature of the welfare state. Only a few politicians in our time would dare to seek election on a platform which absolutely refused to accept any and all features of the welfare state. In this sense, the most significant argument in favor of the welfare state is found not in abstract reasoning, but in the votes of the people. Right or wrong, the people believe that it is possible for the state to intervene in economic matters and by a variety of devices to contribute to the general welfare in a manner and measure unattainable under any other system. Ours appears to be a generation that trusts government.

A number of modern thinkers have arisen to the defense of the welfare state. John Dewey is one of them. He is willing to admit the "apparent intractability of human problems," but he feels that there are resources that have not yet been tried and that these resources carry with them the potential promise of successful application in the large field of human relations. The chief untried resource, in Dewey's opinion, is "the utilization of organized intelligence, the manifold benefits and values of which we have substantial and reliable evidence in the narrower field of science." Thus, Dewey advocates the application of scientific methods in the economic sphere as a means of solving the intractable human problems. The net result of his advocacy is a form of the welfare state.[13]

Not all the advocates of the welfare state are supporters of one form or another of socialism. In fact, the opposite often is true. Russell W. Davenport, for instance, is a strong advocate of social responsibility on the part of businesses. But he concludes that if such organizations are unwilling to meet the challenges presented by the less advantaged in society, the state properly should interfere to meet its social obligation.[14] Similarly, Charles Merriam believes that planning by government is an important ingredient in the preservation of private enterprise. For, as he says, "free enterprise has more to fear from lack of planning than from its development and application to natural resources." [15]

Finally, Arnold J. Toynbee thinks that the idea of the welfare state is so valid and attractive that it would be unfortunate to view it as a luxury, prerogative, or monopoly of the advanced Western nations.[16] Toynbee believes that the welfare state is exportable and that it is an exceedingly attractive promise to the new nations of the world. He wonders how the twentieth century will appear in the prospective of three hundred years. To this he says: "My own guess is that our age will be remembered chiefly neither for its horrifying crimes nor for its astonishing inventions, but for its having been the first age since the dawn of civilization, some five or six thousand years back, in which people dared to think it practicable to make the benefits of civilization available for the whole human race." Toynbee suggests that the common goal must necessarily be approached along different roads because the peoples of the world start their journey toward it from different quarters of the social compass, but the principle he advocates in the achievement of the welfare state for mankind universally is: "a maximum of opportunity for all, combined with a minimum of restriction upon a stronger and wealthier minority's freedom of action." Thus, Toynbee extends the desirability of the welfare state from the advanced nations in Western civilization, where it originated, to the nations, great and small, wealthy and poor, Christian and non-Christian, of the whole world.

The concept of the welfare state, then, depends upon the notion that the state itself possesses an active responsibility for the harmonization or control of the several and even conflicting interests, economically and otherwise, out of which a society forges the greatest degree of human benefit. The welfare state necessarily holds the claims of classical economics with skepticism that the market system is self-regulatory. It also doubts the rational and naïvely sentimental assumptions undergirding both individual and corporate possession of private property. The welfare state, however, rests upon presuppositions that are similar to those enjoyed by classical economics, namely, that by the initiation of rational methods, a highly complex and seemingly nonrational set of activities may be successfully controlled.

The welfare state, as is true of other forms of governmental centralism, raises questions about the nature and extent of individual freedom and the degree to which social institutions other than the state should advance the cause of individual freedom through their quasi-autonomy. This problem was seen clearly, for example, by John Stuart Mill (1806-1873).[17] Mill, with considerable perception, saw that one of the significant dangers concomitant to the development of democratic societies is not that of the domination by wealthy individuals, large corporations or the state. He believed that the greatest threat to individual liberty in the modern world lies in the fact that people "read the same things, listen to the same things, see the same things, go to the same places, have their hopes and fears directed to the same objects, have the same rights and liberties, and the same means of asserting them." He predicted that the economic and political processes under industrialization would lead to a level of conformity which would be stultifying to freedom. Mill stated that conformism in a democratic society is enforced not by individual weakness or acquiescence, but by the assimilation by individuals in groups to their own moral code of the general dictates and standards of the society. Thus, the individual needs to be protected against the tyranny of prevailing opinion as much as against the exercise of political absolutism. Mill's contribution, therefore, is not limited to a criticism of the economic and political sphere of society; it is essentially a message for the totality of the society. The welfare state must heed his analysis and appeal.

DIVIDED RESPONSIBILITIES

At the present time, the development of the welfare state in the United States and elsewhere has left the churches in a dilemma regarding their responsibility for social welfare. The churches are perplexed on two fronts. First, they are currently seeking to reassess the responsibilities for social welfare which uniquely belong to them. Despite the long and varied history of the churches' participation in social welfare activities, the present situation suffers from some confusion. Alan Keith-Lucas, for example, has devoted a volume to the subject.[18]

Second, the churches today are perplexed in connection with their relations with government so far as welfare activities are concerned. The secular promise of the welfare state has been that through the agencies of government the human condition of all citizens would be minimally met and in general advanced to a point that private and religious services would not be required. But the promise has not been fulfilled. The fact is that private and church social service activities have increased as in paralleling fashion the welfare services of government have increased. The expansion of the public services, however, has led some Protestants to have a "sense of uneasiness over the possible threat to democratic and spiritual values implied in the continued expansion of public services."[19]

For this and other reasons, the division of responsibility for welfare services currently constitutes an important aspect of church-state relations.

The "solutions" which have been offered to the dilemma of the relations of church and state in social welfare are many and varied. An exploratory study by the Lutheran Church in America, for example, suggests that there are six fundamental options with regard to governmental action in welfare. These range from the "government should remove itself from the welfare field entirely —except for certain inescapable minimum functions" to the "government should use its power and funds to help create a situation in which public welfare, the service activities of the church, and voluntary welfare are in creative co-operation in serving the needs of persons." [20]

Of course, there are those who, from the standpoint of the churches, rest on the principle of the absolute separation of church and state in social welfare. Such a stand has been expressed by the organization called Protestants and Other Americans United for Separation of Church and State. C. Stanley Lowell, the leader of the organization, emphasizes one clear test. Says Lowell: "Any church seeking tax money for its operations is endeavoring to breach the wall of Church-State separation." [21] The test of money alone, however, is both simple and extreme. This criterion, considered in its direct and indirect phases, is dominantly disregarded by most of the churches.

On the other hand, a theory of relationships between church and state in social welfare responsibilities, often advanced by Roman Catholics, is called subsidiarity. Bernard J. Coughlin defines subsidiarity as follows:

Applied to relationships between government and voluntary agencies, the principle prescribes that where a voluntary association is wholly unequal to its task, the agency must relinquish the task. Where, however, the voluntary association can with help fulfill its responsibility and function, government should extend enabling assistance. Applied in this way, the principle is one of self-determination on the societal level. When, however, government chooses not to give enabling assistance and to take to itself unnecessarily the responsibility and function of such an association, it not only overburdens itself with functions for which it is not equipped, but it also deprives individuals of their right to and need for voluntary association." [22]

If the notion of absolute separation of church and state in welfare responsibilities is less than adequate and seldom practiced, the principle of subsidiarity also has its problems. One, an example of a larger number, has been provided by Dean M. Kelley. It is the disproportional distribution of tax-based resources to public and private hospitals. Kelley describes the situation:

The Hill-Burton Act provides grants for hospital construction through public and private hospitals. Between 1947 and 1963, the program has operated in such a way that public (nonfederal) hospitals, which provided 69 percent of all hospital beds in 1955, got only 43 percent of the Hill-Burton money, while private nonsectarian hospitals, with 19 percent of the beds, got 32 percent of the money. But church-related hospitals, with only 12 percent of the beds, got 25 percent of the money, or twice their share proportionate to existing facilities! [23]

Bernard J. Coughlin concludes a comprehensive and detailed study of church-state relations in social welfare by claiming that a new trend in church-state policy is coming into being. According to Coughlin: "These two strains of influence—church leaders for ideological reasons readapting church policy to the changing social order, and agency administrators for pragmatic reasons determining church policy by actual cooperation with government—are converging to recast the traditional policy of church-state separation." [24] In this claim he well may be correct. Both church and state in their responsibilities for social welfare appear to be ready to acknowledge that each is moving into a new day in which both the churches and the government properly are active in all spheres of life in which human concern is significant. Both church and state appear to recognize that the former time of limited government and individualistic piety are inadequate for the present circumstances. Creative cooperation is the growing rule. Creative cooperation, however, does not mean that church and state should be institutionally fused. Each social institution works best when it is institutionally separate. Each needs in order to be itself the freedom to act, including the freedom to cooperate, where and when it can utilize its resources best for the fulfillment of its institutional objectives. The effect of this cooperative separatism in education, welfare, and community life bears its own dangers and problems, but the assumption is that the other available positions are even more inadequate.

10

Church and State:
The Developing Relationship

THE CHANGED SITUATION

In raising issues regarding the relationships of church and state in American society, one must take into account the current distaste for ideological conflicts. Daniel Bell is right in his claim that the collective experience of the West has reached a point when all vast, encompassing, and doctrinaire systems have lost their power over the minds of men.[1] The situation is particularly apparent in the United States, where major efforts are made to develop professions for the management of differences, although Europe apparently is doing likewise.

But Bell and others are both right and wrong. They are right in thinking that large numbers of people in Europe, America, and elsewhere have a distaste for ideological conflicts. They are wrong, however, in thinking that there are not a host of lively topics on which the liveliest of debates can be based. Consider a few examples: the racial problem everywhere, the Common Market, the new generation of youth, the nature of effective teacher education, inadequate housing, East-West relations, the rising political conservatism in the United States, and a variety of other probing and pressing issues. Certainly the issues involving the relationships between church and state fall squarely into this category, for there are many degrees of literacy apparent in the American scene and a high degree of social unsettlement regarding the causes and consequences of recent modifications of the traditional relationships. On this score, Leo Pfeffer asserts: "More attention has been paid to the subject of Church-State relations by the American people during the past decade and a half than in all the preceding years since the founding of our Republic . . ." [2]

There are a number of complicating factors which make the relationships between church and state in this period in American society particularly vexing. Not all of these factors can be indicated here, but a sampling will, it is hoped, demonstrate the basis on which simple and uncomplicated questions and answers no longer are in vogue.

Pan-Protestantism

First, the passing of the period of pan-Protestantism has significantly modified the over-all problem. Franklin H. Littell has described the transition from the period in American history when the Protestant churches constituted "the establishment" to our time, in which the social situation is often described as one of "pluralism." [3] Yet the period of pan-Protestantism still provides many persons in our society, whether Protestant or not, with a large and important intellectual, social, and legal tradition. Father Robert F. Drinan points to this fact by saying: "Catholics experience special difficulty in making known their convictions, since they must employ terminology not of their own creation and operate within a framework of statutory and decisional law which was designed to protect a pan-Protestant nation from non-Protestant influences." [4] One era has passed, so far as church-state relations are concerned, and another is presently being born.

Meaning of the Church

Second, the various and sometimes conflicting meanings attached to "church" in discussions of church-state relations further complicate the situation. The resulting formulations of the argument often operate on several levels of preciseness. To many people, obviously, to speak of the church is to refer to one's own communion or denomination. But there are many churches in this sense, and the churches are distinguished on the question of church and state by as many differences of opinion as they are on most other subjects. Thus, it is most difficult in America to speak of the "church" without going on to be more specific regarding the exact sense in which the word is used.

The genuine (not merely semantic) confusion in the use of the term "church" was apparent during the Fourth Assembly of the Lutheran World Federation, held in Helsinki on August 11, 1963. Although the assembled Lutherans spoke of *the* Lutheran Church quite often, they could not seriously come to agreement as to the meaning of their usage. Dean F. Clifford Nelson of Luther Seminary in St. Paul, Minnesota, pointed boldly to ecclesiological issues facing Lutherans when he branded as virtually inexcusable the fact that today some of the member churches in the federation do not accord each other pulpit and altar fellowship.

Again, while ecumenism is particularly strong in its international and sloganic developments, it is particularly weak in its expression of unity of opinion and action on such matters as church-state relations.

Meaning of the State

Third, just as there is little agreement regarding the nature of the church, so there is misunderstanding regarding the nature of the state. The fact is that there are many conceptions of the state. The self-legitimizing notion of the state exists in the modern world both in argument and in fact, but the welfare state, a quite different idea and fact, also exists and quite possibly is predominant.

Any discussion of church-state relations in the United States necessarily must take into account the three major levels of government: local, state, and federal. Quite often in the American situation the issues of church and state are most pointed not in regard to the local and federal governments, but in regard to the state governments, since these in general have significant responsibility for such matters as education and marriage, subjects of intense concern to the churches. But the direction of political change in the United States is clearly toward the centralization of government, and the federal government plays an increasingly significant role in many areas that once were reserved to state and local control. The role of the United State Supreme Court, for example, in recent years indicates how significant the federal government has become in the determination of what formerly were considered to be local practices and options.

Religious Vapidity

Fourth, the lack of precise and informed thinking and the lack of vigorous concern on the part of Christians has complicated the situation. Augustus Longstreet, in a study of the Georgia frontier, remarked that "the honest Georgian preferred his whiskey straight and his politics and religion red hot." But that time, if it ever existed, has passed from the life of many Christians today, and it has been gone for some time. Henry Ward Beecher, pastor of Plymouth Congregational Church in Brooklyn from 1847 to 1887, was described by Phillips Brooks as "the greatest preacher of America and of our century." Yet the question "What do you believe?" was ruled out of order in Beecher's church. Lyman Abbott, Beecher's successor in the Plymouth pulpit, boldly stated: "What Mr. Beecher held and this Church holds on this subject, I hold no less earnestly." [5] The rise in religious vapidity has been adequately described by Will Herberg.[6] So today there is a lack of intelligent concern on the part of some Christians in the pressing issues involved in church-state relations.

On this score, it is well to note the considered and informed views of the 174th General Assembly of the United Presbyterian Church in the United States of America. This church's report Relations Between Church and State constitutes the only official and comprehensive statement on church-state relations by an American body. It is significant, therefore, to note that the report stresses the need for the church to think clearly, to maintain its freedom, and to be relevant to society. The United Presbyterian statement also calls upon the church to be the church, saying:

The sole ground for the church's critique of the state is that in Christ, God and the World are reconciled. The witness of the church must take its lead from this fact. To the degree the Christians know this, they have an insight not available to the state, and must call the state to a level of self criticism which it cannot reach alone. However, this presupposes that the church shall sharply maintain itself as a pure witness to Christ. The church can never become so enmeshed in the society that it conforms and becomes unidentifiable as a church. In the heritage of separated church and state the matter can be sharply formulated; not only must each maintain a distinct identity but the church must be itself if the state is to be a state.[7]

All these complicating factors and others have brought the current discussion and analysis of church-state relations to an impasse in which now there is the necessity for Christians as well as others to rethink fundamentally what the proper relationship should be between these two significant social institutions.

INSTITUTIONAL INTERRELATIONS

From a sociological viewpoint, therefore, the relationships between church and state constitute one set of relationships among others. The appropriate satisfaction of human needs depends not upon the dominance of one institution over another, but upon the proper regulation of the existing social institutions so that each is able to perform maximally the purposes for which it exists. It may be claimed, although the claim needs further substantiation, that a democratic society depends upon an efficient differentiation among the several institutions and harmonious relations among them all. Societies, however, tend to develop imbalances among their social institutions. Where the political institution, for example, dominates excessively, a degree of political tyranny exists in which the other social institutions are dwarfed in importance and, therefore, in effectiveness. In other societies the economic interests may achieve such lopsided importance that the full range of institutional practices tends to become subservient to material considerations. Obviously, too, in theocratic societies the social institution of religion dominates, commonly to the detriment of the full blossoming of the other social institutions. It is one of the glories of the present period that the religious institutions are not in a position to dominate all aspects of social life. Freedom for the individual, as well as for his religious group, means in our society that the voluntary principle of group formation is recognized even in the sacred spheres of society.

There is much to be said in favor of constant effort to achieve that form of society in which the several social institutions are afforded the highest degree of autonomous existence. In this sense, the church must be the church and not seek to be the state or any other social institution in society. Similarly, the state must seek to be the state and not in its striving curb the rightful spheres of autonomy which the other social institutions represent.

Yet the separateness and autonomy of the social institutions should not lead to an atomistic society in which special forms lose their significance because of their variety and lack of common coherence.

Emile Durkheim showed the necessity and the benefits

of economic specialization.[8] Some such principle might well be applied to the social institutions in a society, but only to a limited degree, for the tendency to separateness must be counterbalanced by a tendency to commonality. The core forms and values of a society—those which are reflected in the formations of all its social institutions— form the basis on which a society coheres. Paul Tillich is correct in claiming that a society's ethos is fundamentally its religion and vice versa, no matter what the specialized structures and beliefs of the society's social institutions may be.[9] Gerhard Lenski implements this view for the pervasiveness of the Protestant work ethic by showing empirically how cultural norms derived from the social institution of religion are found in measured degree in the economic institutions of Detroit.[10]

A number of the vital issues currently being debated on the subject of church-state relations can be understood in the light of the foregoing discussion of the nature of social institutions. In brief, there are two essentially competitive and conflicting requirements in American life in connection with church-state relations.

First, each social institution must be itself. It must seek to meet those interests and needs from which it has developed and by which it is maintained. The encroachment of one institution upon another not only leads to overt and distressing conflict, but also arises in part from an incomplete or an inadequate understanding of the proper role of each institution in the total society. Affirming the appropriate autonomy of the church and the state is a commendable function of those who value each for its own sake and the welfare of the people as a whole. The danger of encroachment is twofold. Those who accept the importance of religious institutions must show constant alertness to encroachment by the state or by any other social institution. Those who accept the value of the state, however, must ever be on guard lest some other social institution, such as religion, seek a preferred position from which it could dominate the totality of society.

Second, there is another and quite different requirement. Church and state, as well as all of the social institutions, need each other. They cannot withdraw to the castle of their own prerogatives, separated by the moat of vehement self-assertion, to wage warfare against cordial and cooperative relationships that are governed by considerations of the generic need for social coherence and welfare.

These somewhat opposing tendencies must ever be kept in proper balance. There appears to be no dogmatic or universal formula by which the relationships between the social institutions can be regulated. Probably a piecemeal or flexible approach to these relationships is most appropriate to a society which is undergoing rapid social change. There appears to be no special virtue in dogmatic formulations of effective relationships, nor is there any special virtue in the advocacy of the blurring of all distinctions.

THREE FUNDAMENTAL NEEDS

In the light of the complicating factors in the current discussions of church-state relations in American society there exist now a necessity and an opportunity for Christians, along with other citizens, to re-examine the precise nature of the basic issues in the light of the changed situation today.

Also, the realization that the relations between church

and state, from a sociological point of view, are somewhat similar to those among all of the social institutions leads to a basis for the creation of new understanding. The current situation, therefore, calls for the satisfaction of three fundamental needs: (1) the need for a new understanding of the church, (2) the need for a new understanding of the state, and (3) the need for openness to new ideas and forms. These three pressing needs will be briefly reviewed.

THE CHURCH

First, there is need for a new understanding of the church. Dietrich Bonhoeffer states: "The starting-point of St. Paul's thinking is always the Church, and his whole concern is its well-being and manner of life. So much so, he feels obligated to warn the Christians to refrain from any unjust or evil conduct themselves, but does not utter a single word of reproach to the state." [11] If Bonhoeffer is right in thinking that the starting point of the Christian in his understanding of the relationship of the Christian faith to society is the church, then a new understanding of the nature of the church is required in our time.

The constant temptation of Christians in their congregational organizations is to apply material or worldly standards of success, to the detriment of the judging and reconciling work of the spirit in human affairs. But this tendency to converge Christianity into a culture religion is as old as the earthly ministry of Jesus, and has been apparent in every historical period since that time. One is reminded, for example, of the response by which C. C. McCabe of the Methodist Church Extension Society sought to answer the taunt of Robert G. Ingersoll: "The

Churches are dying out all over the land." McCabe sent the following telegram to Ingersoll: "Dear Robert: 'All hail the power of Jesus' name'—we are building more than one Methodist Church for every day in the year and propose to make it two a day! C. C. McCabe." [12] The notion that the reconciling power of Jesus in personal and social life can be expressed adequately through a questionable and pretentious building program causes many sincere Christians today to be tempted to despair. Yet "extension" efforts of the past have been dwarfed by the activities of the Protestant communions in the post-Second World War period. Thus, Christians seem even eager at times to equate the nature of their religious faith with worldly standards of success.

The Christian churches, unfortunately, have progressively lost their "sect" character and have became absorbed in the engulfing secular culture of America. This development has occurred at just that juncture in American history when religiously authentic and socially critical churches are sorely needed. Reinhold Niebuhr wrote perceptively in 1947: "Whatever the weaknesses of the 'sectarian' church which has set the pattern for American church life, one should think that the prevailing secularism of modern culture might give the idea of an exclusive church new validity." Niebuhr's observation underscores the importance of the development of a true understanding of the church.

A number of critics have arisen in recent years to lambast the churches for their failure to avoid material or worldly standards of effectiveness. Gibson Winter and Peter Berger are two of the more popular critics.[13] Criticism is indeed needed, yet it should not obscure the adaptiveness of the churches to the problems that their critics describe. On this score, one needs historical perspective. At the beginning of the nineteenth century, to select only one example, the churches seem to have fallen into a period of weakness within a society characterized by significant economic evils, the failure of conscience to challenge the evil of property, and similar social ills. But it is significant that it was in this very period that a variety of new forms arose on a national basis under church leadership to meet the social and religious crisis. Some of these national organizations were the American Bible Society (1816), the American Colonization Society (1817), the American Sunday School Union (1824), the American Temperance Society (1826), the American Home Missionary Society (1826), the American Education Society (1827), the American Peace Society (1828), the American Seaman's Friend Society (1828), the American Tract Society (1828), the American Anti-Slavery Society (1833), and others too numerous to mention.[14] The American churches in that period of social crisis overcame their tendency to lethargy and produced a variety of socially significant efforts that contributed richly to the redemption of the worst features of American life.

So in our time, faced as we are by a variety of genuinely distressing social problems and with many churches virtually moribund in their accommodation of material and worldly standards, there exists the fresh and lively development of new concerns and new forms of Christian expression. The most obvious instance of this renewal is the widespread concern among Christians, both as individuals and through organizations, for the marshaling of Christian resources for the alleviation of the plight of Negro citizens and for urban renewal.

The nature of the church in its organizational and cultural expressions has never been static. In its response to the divine initiative it must constantly seek to express itself in new forms. By such expression a new understanding of the church results. At present, there appears to be a need for the understanding not only of the church as it is but of the church as it must be in a community of God-oriented persons in a tragic and torn era.

The State

Second, there is need for a new understanding of the state. Paradoxically, adequate explanations of the nature of a social institution often lie in ranges of theory and value beyond it. Social institutions have a notable tendency to be self-justifying. Being conservative, they are attracted to explanations of their natures which tend to enhance their autonomy and power. The rationale supporting the so-called free enterprise system of economics, for example, has led on occasion, as has Marxian economics, to metaphysical assumptions and assertions that are not supported by the daily practices within the social institution. Similarly, the world knows well enough the demonic power of political institutions which are self-justifying in the extreme. Nazism may have been based in part upon a theory of race, but in its political manifestations it tended to place intolerable power in the state. Communism may originally have been based upon an explanation of the nature of the economy, but in its political manifestations it, too, has garnered an amazing degree of political dominance over all other social institutions under its sway.

The new understanding of the nature of the state must,

in part at least, derive from suppositions, theories, and values which are beyond the state, that is, which are not a consequence of in-group thinking. A strong system of values which are independent of the state is needed in any society which seeks to avoid political extremism. Distinctly religious values may not be the only source by which a society can resist the development of political extremism, but as Seymour Lipset remarks: "Social systems undergoing major institutional changes, which weaken faith in traditional religion and which do not replace this lost faith by the value system of an open achievement-oriented society, have experienced major extremist political movement." [15]

One of the dangers of the present-day secularity lies essentially at this point. Secularism, as it has been known historically, simply does not have the power within itself to transcend the self-justifying tendencies of the social institutions. Traditional religion, as Lipset acknowledges, could have that power; and to those who acknowledge its validity today, it continues to be a significant source of resistance to the absolutizing of any social institution, particularly of the state.

There is also need for a new understanding of the state as an obligation of Christian theology. Christians cannot agree among themselves regarding the proper role of the state in the creation of the orders of society by man and God and in the redemption of man and society by the power of the New Creation, and they cannot rest until the matter is grappled with. And, in fact, the subject is currently one of considerable concern among Christian theologians. Dietrich Bonhoeffer has examined the subject in several of his books, and declares in *The Cost of Dis-*

cipleship that the Pauline doctrine of the state in Romans 13 is highly illuminating.[16] Karl Barth also has dealt extensively with the subject in his writings, and concludes in his *Community, State, and Church* that the relations between church and state cannot be properly understood without an understanding of the three orders of created being: (1) the "order of creation," defining the order of life for which God created man and which he intends him to live; (2) the "order of preservation," consisting of the forms and institutions of social life made necessary by human sinfulness, that is, by man's proneness to make himself the center of this universe and to subject others to his will, and designed to protect human life in society from the ravages of sin; and (3) the "order of redemption," which mediates the saving word of God to man estranged and lost in his sinfulness. Thus, to Barth the state is made necessary by man's sinful urge to self-aggrandizement at the expense of others. As such, it is part of the "order of preservation." He asserts, however, that the state has a tendency to go beyond its proper calling by "sacralizing" itself, by converting itself into its own highest majesty, and making total claims upon the individual, demanding his soul as well as his body. The sacralized state, in Barth's view, is not entitled to respect or obedience. It is like the "beast out of the abyss" of Revelation 13.[17]

John C. Bennett also has written widely on the subject, and his book *Christians and the State* embodies many of his views on the nature of the state. Bennett is deeply appreciative of the position of the Christian faith in a religiously pluralistic society. In such a society, he thinks, the citizenry must depend upon an existing moral consensus by which the social life of man is maintained with the required degree of coherence and meaning. He is impressed with the idea of balancing power in government, particularly as it has been developed in the government of the United States, and finds in the concepts of the "limited state" considerable virtue from the standpoints of both justice and morality.[18]

Obviously, other distinguished theologians are grappling with the problem of the nature of the state. Although they are at times distressingly confused and conflicting in their opinions, in general they are helping to develop a new understanding of the state.

Yet the greater part of the work of creating new understanding lies ahead. In this regard it is more possible now to say what the state should not be than to assert and describe its positive features. Thus, Christians and others are able to say "No" to Edmund Burke when he says: "It is in the power of government to prevent much evil; it can do very little positive good in this, or perhaps in anything else." Christians also are able to say "No" even to Martin Luther, who proclaimed: "The princes of this world are gods; the common people are Satans through whom God sometimes does what at other times He does directly through Satan." Christians and others, moreover, say a resounding "No" to Jean-Jacques Rousseau when he speaks in terms of the organic analogy: "The social pact gives the body politic an absolute power over all its members." Christians and others can say "No" to all these sentiments and others, although they may be hard put to provide a satisfactory and positive description, especially from the stance of the Christian faith, of the new understanding of the state which is essential for the present age.

Openness

Third, there is need for openness to new ideas and forms. The constantly changing character of the state and of the church calls for openness to new ideas and forms. There is some evidence that partisans on both sides of the issues of church-state relations are viewing both the church and the state in outworn and inadequate ways. To many, the terms "church" and "state" tend to take on absolutized meanings which are unworthy of the complicated situation in which such issues need to be discussed. A process similar to "demythologizing" needs to be undertaken in connection with these sloganic expressions. How much obscurity has been created through the use of the simple phrase "the separation of church and state"! The time has come, and indeed is past, when Christians and others must look behind and beyond the facades of tired and unilluminating words. As Evarts B. Greene states: "Now, however, in these middle years of the twentieth century, we begin to suspect that certain age-old problems are not so simple as they once seemed." [19]

Openness to new ideas and forms also should preclude little-mindedness. Too often the big guns of extremism are brought to bear upon problems of little consequence. Thus, in July, 1966, the Postmaster General's office received strong protests against the issuance of a 1966 Christmas stamp reproducing a Madonna and Child. The reproduction was to be of a segment of a Hans Memling painting that hangs in the National Gallery in Washington. But religious leaders and others claimed that the painting was religious in nature and that its reproduction on a postage stamp violated the Constitutional separation of church and state. In rejecting the protest, the Postmaster General's office contended that no one was forced to use the Christmas stamp. The rejection noted that postmasters had other issues, regular and commemorative, for patrons who preferred them.[20] Similarly, the Census Bureau in August, 1966, expressed doubt that it would require citizens to specify their religion in the 1970 census, on the grounds that there were strong protests from those who contend that such a query would deprive persons of religious liberty. The bureau has long been interested in collecting information on religion, but it has never done so because of heavy opposition. It seriously considered collecting such data in 1960 for the first time, but dropped the idea because of criticism. From these and other instances it would appear that openness to new ideas and forms should mean that petty issues will not becloud social wisdom.

If one major way of obscuring the proper relations between church and state is to take refuge in slogans, another method is merely to consider the issues of church-state relations as essentially "court" problems. There has been an obvious tendency in recent years to reduce the permanent and significant issues between church and state to a subject of constitutional history and decision. The fact that the recent decisions of the United States Supreme Court on church-state cases have been so widely resented in the population is due in part to the Court's inexplicable unawareness of the interplay between constitutional rights and the social realities in this area. The United States Supreme Court inconsistently bows to the old pieties while at the same time it fumblingly attempts to come to terms with the new social realities. The Court, like the citizenry, is caught in the anomalous situation of a nation that almost universally supports tax exemption for churches, governmental and military chaplaincies, prayers in the Congress and in the courts (if no longer in the public schools), proclamations of days of prayer and thanksgiving by the president, and federal grants to sectarian colleges and universities while some of its members talk the language of an absolutist "separation of church and state." These inconsistencies cannot ultimately be resolved merely through actions of the Court. They are deeply imbedded in American life, and ultimately can be resolved only by an openness to the creation of new ideas and forms by which church and state will be constructively related to each other, not only for their own benefit but for the welfare of all. Some of the issues of church-state relations may be resolved through the action of the courts, but the courts can never address themselves to the full range of issues which are apparent in the culture of America.

The preoccupation of many Americans, both as individuals and in organizations, with the constitutionality of legislation and administrative action has grown in the recent years to an astonishing degree. Substantial efforts have been required to codify and understand the actions of the courts on constitutional matters. Sam Duker, for example, has examined the legal context of religion and the public schools at length and in detail.[21] Similarly, Joseph Tussman has edited a book on the many decisions of the United States Supreme Court on the subject of church and state.[22] Other volumes and special studies have sought to keep track of and understand the multitudinous considerations by the courts on the theme of church and state.[23] The courts in part form social policy, but their primary aim is to establish the legitimacy of social behavior in the light of the restraint of rule and principle. The courts have no mandated function of advocating what truly should be. This function must be assumed by other social institutions in society.

Church-state relationships in the United States are undergoing change. The fact is, moreover, that the relationships have never been entirely stable. Those who feel threatened by change, whether individuals or groups, will see danger in the present situation. Others will view the present era as providing an opportunity to give up the inadequacies of the past and to push on toward a perfection not yet known. In this regard, the sentiments of Franklin H. Littell are pertinent:

America is called to become a world city, a meeting place of the peoples. Even the reform movements of Islam, Buddhism, and Hinduism, once ethnic religions, are sending missionaries to the great cities of North America. The style of a universal spirit of dialogue is replacing the old order of coercion and arbitrament by the knife. The mind locked in a fortress, defending an ethnic complex called "Christendom," would resist such encounter by writ and by law. The mind that is fearless in faith and open to the dialogue will welcome it; it will accept the truth that a religion that cannot win its case and grow on its merit is unworthy of the future. The churches will continue to influence the form and direction of the world city, perhaps more than they did during the time when the pluralism of loyalties was hidden behind a facade of established orthodoxy. But they will earn the right to be heard by their evidence of internal integrity and interreligious amity. They will no longer inherit the right to rule.[24]

Author's Notes

PREFACE

1. Herbert Stroup, "Church and State in American Society," *Social Action*, Vol. 30, No. 3 (Nov., 1963), pp. 6-21.

CHAPTER 1: THE PROBLEM
OF CHURCH-STATE RELATIONSHIPS

1. Thomas Jefferson, *The Complete Jefferson: Containing His Major Writings, Published and Unpublished Except His Letters,* assembled and arranged by Saul K. Padover (New York: Duell, Sloan and Pearce, 1943), pp. 538-539.

2. Sidney E. Mead, *The Lively Experiment: The Shaping of Christianity in America* (New York: Harper and Row, 1963).

3. Kenneth Scott Latourette, *A History of the Expansion of Christianity* (New York: Harper, 1962), Vol. IV, p. 424.

4. Winfred E. Garrison, "Characteristics of American Organized Religion," *Annals of the American Academy of Political and Social Science,* Vol. 155 (Mar., 1948), p. 17.

5. 1 Thessalonians 4:13-18.

6. Philippians 1:23-24; 2 Timothy 4:6-8.

7. Paul Tillich, *Theology of Culture,* ed. Robert C. Kimball (New York: Oxford University Press, 1959), p. 42.

8. H. Richard Niebuhr, *Christ and Culture* (New York: Harper, 1951), esp. pp. 1-44.

9. Alfred North Whitehead, *Process and Reality: An Essay in Cosmology* (New York: Macmillan, 1930), p. 327.

10. Robert McAfee Brown, "Types of Anti-Catholicism," *Commonweal,* Vol. 63 (Nov. 25, 1955), pp. 193-196.

11. John C. Bennett, *Christians and the State* (New York: Scribners, 1958), p. 205.

12. Sam Duker, *The Public Schools and Religion: The Legal Context* (New York: Harper and Row, 1966), p. 228.

13. Commission on Church and State Relations in a Pluralistic Society, *Church and State: A Lutheran Perspective: The Interaction of Re-*

ligion and Law in a Pluralistic Society (New York: Board of Social Ministry, Lutheran Church in America, 1963), pp. 36-41.

14. Bronislaw Malinowski, "The Group and the Individual in Functional Analysis," *The American Journal of Sociology*, Vol. 44 (May, 1939), pp. 938-964; also "Culture" in *Encyclopaedia of the Social Sciences*, Vol. 4, pp. 621-645.

15. Joyce Hertzler, *Social Institutions* (Lincoln: University of Nebraska Press, 1946).

16. Donald G. Miller, *The Nature and Mission of the Church* (Richmond: John Knox Press, 1957), p. 17.

17. H. Paul Douglass and Edmund deS. Brunner, *The Protestant Church as a Social Institution* (New York: Institute of Social and Religious Research, 1935), pp. 13-15.

18. Walter G. Muelder, "From Sect to Church," *Christendom*, Vol. 10 (Autumn, 1945), pp. 453-454.

CHAPTER 2: CHANGING PERSPECTIVES:
THE CHURCH

1. William Lee Miller, "Religion and the American Way of Life," *Religion and the Free Society* (New York: The Fund for the Republic, 1958), pp. 18-19.

2. Sidney E. Mead, *The Lively Experiment: The Shaping of Christianity in America* (New York: Harper and Row, 1963), p. 103.

3. Winfred E. Garrison, "Characteristics of American Organized Religion," *Annals of the American Academy of Political and Social Science*, Vol. 256 (Mar., 1948), pp. 14-24; and W. W. Sweet, *The American Churches* (New York: Abingdon-Cokesbury Press, 1948), pp. 8, 110-149.

4. H. Paul Douglass and Edmund deS. Brunner, *The Protestant Church as a Social Institution* (New York: Institute of Social and Religious Research, 1935), pp. 139-146.

5. *From Max Weber: Essays in Sociology*, ed. Hans H. Gerth and C. Wright Mills (New York: Oxford University Press, 1946), pp. 287-288, 305-306, 313-319.

6. *From Max Weber: Essays in Sociology*, ed. Hans H. Gerth and C. Wright Mills (New York: Oxford University Press, 1946), pp. 287-288, 305-306, 313-319.

7. Ernst Troeltsch, *The Social Teaching of the Christian Churches*, trans. Olive Wyon (New York: Macmillan, 1931), Vol. I, p. 336.

8. Ernst Troeltsch, *The Social Teaching of the Christian Churches*, trans. Olive Wyon (New York: Macmillan, 1931), Vol. II, p. 995.

9. Joachim Wach, *Sociology of Religion* (Chicago: University of Chicago Press, 1944).

10. J. Milton Yinger, *Religion, Society and the Individual: An Introduction to the Sociology of Religion* (New York: Macmillan, 1957), pp. 147-148.

11. Howard Becker, *Through Values to Social Interpretation: Essays on Social Contexts, Actions, Types and Prospects* (Durham: Duke University Press, 1950), pp. 114-118.

12. J. Milton Yinger, *Religion, Society and the Individual: An Introduction to the Sociology of Religion* (New York: Macmillan, 1957), pp. 147-155.

13. H. Richard Niebuhr, *The Social Sources of Denominationalism* (New York: Holt, 1929).

14. H. Richard Niebuhr, *The Social Sources of Denominationalism* (New York: Holt, 1929), pp. 16-17.

15. Anton T. Boisen, "Divided Protestantism in a Midwest County; A Study in the Natural History of Organized Religion," *Journal of Religion*, Vol. 20 (October, 1940), pp. 359-381.

16. Elmer T. Clark, *The Small Sects in America* (New York: Abingdon-Cokesbury Press, 1949).

17. Emile Durkheim, *The Division of Labor in Society*, trans. George Simpson (Glencoe: Free Press, 1947), p. 169.

18. Gordon W. Allport, James M. Gillespie, and Jacqueline Young, "The Religion of the Post-War College Student," *The Journal of Psychology*, Vol. 25 (1948), pp. 3-33.

19. Harvey Cox, *The Secular City: Secularization and Urbanization in Theological Perspective* (New York: Macmillan, 1965), pp. 2-3.

20. Daniel Callahan, ed., *The Secular City Debate* (New York: Macmillan, 1966).

21. John C. Bennett, *Christians and the State* (New York: Scribners, 1958), p. 5.

22. John C. Bennett, *Christians and the State* (New York: Scribners, 1958), p. 258.

23. H. Richard Niebuhr, *The Purpose of the Church and Its Ministry* (New York: Harper, 1956), p. 90.

24. Paul M. Harrison, *Authority and Power in the Free Church Tradition: A Social Study of the American Baptist Convention* (Princeton: Princeton University Press, 1959), chs. 4-5.

25. Harvey Cox, *The Secular City: Secularization and Urbanization in Theological Perspective* (New York: Macmillan, 1965), p. 21.

26. Harvey Cox, *The Secular City: Secularization and Urbanization in Theological Perspective* (New York: Macmillan, 1965), pp. 20-21.

27. James Hastings Nichols, *Democracy and the Churches* (Philadelphia: Westminster Press, 1951), esp. ch. 1.

28. Franklin H. Littell, *From State Church to Pluralism: A Protestant Interpretation of Religion in American History* (Garden City: Anchor Books, 1962).

29. Franklin H. Littell, *From State Church to Pluralism: A Protestant Interpretation of Religion in American History* (Garden City: Anchor Books, 1962), p. 17.

30. Franklin H. Littell, *From State Church to Pluralism: A Protestant Interpretation of Religion in American History* (Garden City: Anchor Books, 1962), pp. 163-164.

31. Franklin H. Littell, *From State Church to Pluralism: A Protestant Interpretation of Religion in American History* (Garden City: Anchor Books, 1962), p. 167.

32. Andrew M. Greeley and Peter H. Rossi, *The Education of Catholic Americans* (Chicago: Aldine, 1966).

CHAPTER 3: CHANGING PERSPECTIVES:
THE STATE

1. Karl Polanyi, *The Great Transformation* (New York: Farrar and Rinehart, 1944).

2. See, for example, Reinhold Niebuhr, *The Children of Light and the Children of Darkness: A Vindication of Democracy and a Critique of Traditional Defence* (New York: Scribners, 1947).

3. *The Republic of Plato* (New York: E. P. Dutton, 1940).

4. Georg Wilhelm Friedrich Hegel, *The Philosophy of History* (New York: Dover Publications, 1956).

5. Bertrand Russell, *Philosophy and Politics* (Cambridge: Cambridge University Press, 1947).

6. René de Visme Williamson, "The Challenge of Political Relativism," *The Journal of Politics*, Vol. 9 (May, 1947), pp. 147-178.

7. *Herodotus*, with an English translation by A. D. Godley, the Loeb Classical Library (New York: G. P. Putnam, 1928), Vol. II, Book 3, chs. 80-83, pp. 105-111.

8. Plato, *The Republic*, books VIII and IX.

9. Aristotle, *Politics*, books III and IV; *Nicomachean Ethics*, Book VIII, where instead of "polity" he speaks of "timocracy."

10. Benedict de Spinoza, *Tractatus Politicus*, Book VIII.

11. Cicero, *De Republica*, Book I, Sec. 26.

12. Thomas Aquinas, *Summa Theologica*, Book II, 1.q. 95, a.4, and q. 105, a.1.

13. Walt Rostow, *The Stages of Economic Growth: A Non-Communist Manifesto* (London: Cambridge University Press, 1960).

14. Zbigniew Brzezinski and Samuel P. Huntington, *Political Power: USA/USSR*, (New York: Viking Press, 1964), p. 420.

15. Robert M. MacIver, *The Web of Government* (New York: Macmillan, 1947), pp. 151-162.

16. Plato, *The Republic*, Book IX.

17. An example of a religious leader opposing the decision of the Court is Charles Wesley Lowry, *To Pray or not to Pray* (Washington: The University Press of Washington, D.C., 1963); other sources are also available on the subject of the First Amendment and the decisions of the Court: Philip B. Kurland, *Religion and the Law of Church and State and the Supreme Court* (Chicago: Aldine, 1962); Dallin H. Oaks, ed., *The Wall Between Church and State* (Chicago: University of Chicago Press, 1963); William H. Marnell, *The First Amendment: The History of Religious Freedom in America* (Garden City: Doubleday, 1964).

18. *The New York Times Magazine* (Dec. 9, 1951).

19. Quoted in James O'Neill, *Catholicism and American Freedom* (New York: Harper, 1952) , p. 61.

20. Perry Miller, "The Religious Impulse in the Founding of Virginia: Religion and Society in the Early Literature," *William and Mary Quarterly*, Third Series, Vol. 5 (Oct., 1948), p. 510, quoted in Sidney E. Mead, *The Lively Experiment: The Shaping of Christianity in America* (New York: Harper and Row, 1963), pp. 77-78.

21. J. Milton Yinger, *Religion in the Struggle for Power* (Durham: Duke University Press, 1946).

22. *Religion and American Society: A Statement of Principles* (Santa Barbara: Center for the Study of Democratic Institutions, 1961), p. 55.

CHAPTER 4: CHURCH-STATE IN THE BIBLE

1. William Temple, *Nature, Man and God* (New York: St. Martin's Press, 1953), p. 500.

2. Special Committee on Church and State, *Relations Between Church and State* (Philadelphia: Office of the General Assembly, 1962), p. 6.

3. For example, Williston Walker, *A History of the Christian Church* (New York: Scribners, 1959).

4. For example, Franklin H. Littell, *From State Church to Pluralism: A Protestant Interpretation of Religion in American History* (Garden City: Anchor Books, 1962).

5. For example, Max Weber, *The Protestant Ethic and the Spirit of Capitalism* (New York: Scribners, 1948).

6. A useful compendium of theory and research is David O. Moberg, *The Church as a Social Institution: The Sociology of American Religion* (Englewood Cliffs: Prentice-Hall, 1962).

7. James M. Gustafson, *Treasure in Earthen Vessels: The Church as a Human Community* (New York: Harper, 1961), p. 14.

8. James M. Gustafson, *Treasure in Earthen Vessels: The Church as a Human Community* (New York: Harper, 1961), pp. 14-15.

9. For example, Karl Barth, *Community, State, and Church* (Garden City: Anchor Books, 1960).

10. James M. Gustafson, *Treasure in Earthen Vessels: The Church as a Human Community* (New York: Harper, 1961), p. 100.

11. Hebrews 8:8. All quotations in this chapter are from the Revised Standard Version.

12. Philippians 3:3.

13. Romans 4:16-25.

14. Ephesians 2:12.

15. Galatians 6:16.

16. 1 Peter 1:1.

17. Mark 12:29-30.

18. Exodus 19:5-6.

19. Psalms 22:27-28.

20. Isaiah 42:6-7.

21. Exodus 19:23.

22. Joshua 7:1.
23. Deuteronomy 7:7-8.
24. Jeremiah 31:3.
25. Jeremiah 11:4.
26. Exodus 24:7.
27. Micah 4:7ff.
28. Zechariah 8:6, 11ff.
29. Jeremiah 31:31-33.
30. Jeremiah 31:32.
31. Jeremiah 31:33.
32. Jeremiah 31:33.
33. 1 Corinthians 11:30.
34. Revelation 1:10.
35. 1 Corinthians 1:2.
36. Acts 20:28.
37. 2 John 1:13.
38. 1 Corinthians 3:16; Ephesians 2:21; 1 Timothy 3:15; Hebrews 10:21; Revelation 3:12.
39. Romans 12:5; 1 Corinthians 12:27; Ephesians 1:23, 4:12, 5:30; Colossians 1:18, 24.
40. Mark 3:33-35.
41. Mark 10:29-30.
42. Matthew 13:24-30, 36-43, 47-50.
43. Matthew 22:1-14.
44. Matthew 16:18; 18:18.
45. Matthew 18:15-17.
46. Revelation 1:6; 5:10.
47. 1 Peter 2:5, 9.
48. 1 Timothy 3:15.
49. Genesis 14:13-16; Judges 11:5; 1 Samuel 30:26.
50. Exodus 18:13-26.
51. Exodus 24:3-8; Deuteronomy, Chapter 27; Joshua 24:1-28.
52. Deuteronomy 19:12; 2 Kings 10:1.
53. Deuteronomy 16:18.
54. 1 Chronicles 11:14.
55. Judges 4:4ff.; Exodus 18:13.
56. 1 Samuel 7:15-17.
57. Judges, Chapter 8ff.
58. Deuteronomy 17:14ff.
59. 2 Samuel 5:12.
60. 1 Samuel 15:23.
61. 1 Kings 12:16.
62. 1 Kings 12:16.
63. 2 Kings 9:1-28.
64. Mark 10:42-45.
65. Judges 9:8-15.
66. 1 Samuel 10:6, 10; 11:6; 16ff.
67. 1 Samuel 9:26ff.; 16:1-13.
68. 1 Kings 1:39; 2 Kings 11:12.

69. 1 Samuel 11:15; 2 Samuel 2:4; 5:3.

70. 1 Kings 1:5-53; 2 Samuel 7:12-16; Psalms 89:3ff.

71. 1 Samuel, Chapter 15.

72. 2 Samuel 12:7-12; 1 Kings 1:26-40; 1 Kings, Chapters 17-19; 21.

73. A concise and definitive analysis of the New Testament understanding of the state may be found in Oscar Cullmann, *The State in the New Testament* (New York: Scribners, 1956).

74. Matthew 26:52; Luke 22:36.

75. Matthew 4:8ff. Luke 4:5-7.

76. Luke 6:15; Acts 1:13.

77. Matthew 11:12; Luke 16:16.

78. Acts, Chapter 12.

79. Romans 13:1-7.

80. 1 Peter 2:13-17.

81. Revelation, Chapter 13:11-18.

82. Revelation 17:1-6.

CHAPTER 5: CHURCH-STATE
IN WESTERN HISTORY

1. John C. Bennett, *Christians and the State* (New York: Scribners, 1958), p. ix.

2. H. Richard Niebuhr, *Christ and Culture* (New York: Harper, 1951).

3. Joachim Wach, *Sociology of Religion* (Chicago: University of Chicago Press, 1944), ch. 7, pp. 287-330.

4. J. Milton Yinger, *Religion, Society and the Individual: An Introduction to the Sociology of Religion* (New York: Macmillan, 1957), pp. 243-245.

5. David O. Moberg, *The Church as a Social Institution: The Sociology of American Religion* (Englewood Cliffs: Prentice-Hall, 1962), pp. 368-369.

6. Murray S. Stedman, Jr., *Religion and Politics in America* (New York: Harcourt, Brace and World, 1964), ch. 4.

7. Anson Phelps Stokes, *Church and State in the United States*, 3 vols. (New York: Harper, 1950), pp. 37-49.

8. Thomas G. Sanders, *Protestant Concepts of Church and State: Historical Backgrounds and Approaches for the Future* (New York: Holt, Rinehart and Winston, 1964).

9. A significant number of specialized studies on church-state relations, particularly national and historical contexts, are available. The following are instructive: Paul P. Anderson, *People, Church and State in Modern Russia* (New York: Macmillan, 1944); Wilfrid H. Callcott, *Church and State in Mexico; 1822-1857* (New York: Octagon Books, 1926); John Shelton Curtiss, *Church and State in Russia: The Last Years of the Empire: 1900-1917* (New York: Columbia University Press, 1940); Arthur H. Galton, *Church and State in France: 1300-1907* (London: E. Arnold, 1907); Cyril Forster Garbett, *Church and State in England* (London: Hodder and Stoughton, 1950); Vladimir Gsovski, *Church and State Behind the Iron Curtain* (New York: Frederick A. Praeger, 1955); Ernst

Helmreich, ed., *A Free Church in a Free Society?: The Catholic Church: Italy, Germany, France, 1864-1914* (Boston: D. C. Heath, 1964); Mary P. Holleran, *Church and State in Guatemala* (New York: Columbia University Press, 1949); Charles B. Kinney, *Church and State; The Struggle for Separation in New Hampshire* (New York: Teachers College, Columbia University, 1953); John L. Mecham, *Church and State in Latin America: A History of Politico-Ecclesiastical Relations* (Chapel Hill: University of North Carolina Press, 1934); Karl F. Morrison. *The Two Kingdoms: Ecclesiology in Carolingian Political Thought* (Princeton: Princeton University Press, 1964); Fredrick B. Pike, ed., *The Conflict Between Church and State in Latin America* (New York: Knopf, 1964); Gustav Schnurer, *Church and Culture in the Middle Ages* (Paterson: St. Anthony Guild Press, 1956); Arthur L. Smith, *Church and State in the Middle Ages* (London: Oxford University Press, 1938); Richard Solberg, *God and Man in East Germany* (New York: Macmillan, 1960); Matthew Spinka, *The Church in Soviet Russia* (New York: Oxford University Press, 1956); Anson Phelps Stokes, *Church and State in the United States*, 3 vols. (New York: Harper, 1950); Leicester C. Webb, *Church and State in Italy: 1947-1957* (Melbourne: Melbourne University Press, 1958). Other volumes that provide historical information are given in the notes throughout the book.

10. Thomas Ford Hoult, *The Sociology of Religion* (New York: Holt, Rinehart and Winston, 1958), p. 59.

11. Langdon Gilkey, "Social and Intellectual Sources of Contemporary Protestant Theology in America," *Dædalus* (Winter, 1967), p. 76.

12. Langdon Gilkey, "Social and Intellectual Sources of Contemporary Protestant Theology in America," *Dædelus* (Winter, 1967), p. 80.

13. Lloyd W. Warner, *American Life: Dream and Reality* (Chicago: University of Chicago Press, 1962), pp. 2-3.

14. W. Robertson Smith, *Lectures on the Religion of the Semites* (3d ed., London: Black, 1927), p. 32.

15. Hermann Doerries, *Constantine and Religious Liberty* (New Haven: Yale University Press, 1960).

16. A scholarly survey of church-state problems, the solutions proposed, the arguments for and against, are described from a constitutional-legal standpoint and in advocacy of "strict" or maximum separation of church and state by Leo Pfeffer, *Church, State, and Freedom* (Boston: Beacon Press, 1953).

17. *Fortune* (Jan., 1940), p. 26.

18. A. Roy Eckhardt, *The Surge of Piety in America* (New York: Association Press, 1958).

19. Martin E. Marty, *The New Shape of American Religion* (New York: Harper and Row, 1959).

20. Will Herberg, *Protestant, Catholic, Jew; An Essay in American Religious Sociology* (Garden City: Doubleday, 1955).

21. Ralph Lord Roy, *Apostles of Discord* (Boston: Beacon Press, 1953).

22. Reinhold Niebuhr, *Reflections on the End of an Era* (New York: Scribners, 1934), pp. 183-184.

23. Daniel Bell, *The End of Ideology* (Glencoe: Free Press, 1960), p. 28.

24. Augustine, *The City of God*, trans. Marcus Dods (New York: Modern Library, 1950), Book 14, para. 28, p. 477.

25. Augustine, *The City of God*, trans. Marcus Dods (New York: Modern Library, 1950), Book 20, para. 9, pp. 725-726.

26. Harry Emerson Fosdick, *Great Voices of the Reformation: An Anthology* (New York: Modern Library, 1952), pp. 289-290.

27. A reassertion of the Anabaptist-Mennonite vision of independent congregations, voluntarily serving under the discipline of their faith, has been composed by Franklin H. Littell, *The Free Church* (Boston: Beacon Press, 1957).

28. Guy F. Hershberger, *War, Peace, and Non-Resistance* (Scottdale, Pa.: Herald Press, 1944), p. 189; quoted in Thomas G. Sanders, *Protestant Concepts of Church and State: Historical Backgrounds and Approaches for the Future* (New York: Holt, Rinehart and Winston, 1964), p. 97.

CHAPTER 6: CHURCH-STATE IN WESTERN HISTORY (CONTINUED)

1. J. Marcellus Kik, *Church and State; The Story of Two Kingdoms* (New York: Thomas Nelson and Sons, 1963).

2. Karl F. Morrison, *The Two Kingdoms: Ecclesiology in Carolingian Political Thought* (Princeton: Princeton University Press, 1964).

3. H. Richard Niebuhr, *Christ and Culture* (New York: Harper, 1951), pp. 149 ff.

4. Martin Luther, "On Secular Authority," *Works of Martin Luther* (Philadelphia: Muhlenberg, 1930), Vol. III, pp. 234, 236.

5. Martin Luther, "Whether Soldiers, Too, Can Be Saved," *Works of Martin Luther* (Philadelphia: Muhlenberg, 1930), Vol. V, p. 39.

6. Martin Luther, "Eighty-second Psalm," *Works of Martin Luther* (Philadelphia: Muhlenberg, 1930), Vol. IV, pp. 297-298.

7. Commission on Church and State Relations in a Pluralistic Society, *Church and State: A Lutheran Perspective* (New York: Board of Social Ministry, Lutheran Church in America, 1963).

8. Albert D. Huegli, ed., *Church and State Under God* (St. Louis: Concordia, 1964).

9. See, for example, Joseph H. Fichter, *Social Relations in the Urban Parish* (Chicago: University of Chicago Press, 1954), pp. 182-184.

10. *The New York Times* (Aug. 25, 1964), p. 29.

11. *People* v. *Woody*, 61 Cal. 2d 716, 394P. 2d 813, 821-22, 1964.

12. Reinhold Niebuhr, *The Nature and Destiny of Man: A Christian Interpretation* (New York: Scribners, 1945), Vol. II, p. 70.

13. Willard L. Sperry, *Religion in America* (New York: Macmillan, 1946), pp. 195-196.

14. William G. McLoughlin, "Is There a Third Force in Christendom?," *Dædalus* (Winter, 1967), p. 62.

15. Joseph R. Washington, Jr., *Black Religion: The Negro and Christianity in the United States* (Boston: Beacon Press, 1964).

16. Max Weber, *From Max Weber: Essays in Sociology,* ed. and trans. H. H. Gerth and C. Wright Mills (New York: Oxford University Press, 1946), p. 336.

17. H. Richard Niebuhr, *Christ and Culture* (New York: Harper, 1951), pp. 190 ff.

18. H. Richard Niebuhr, *Christ and Culture* (New York: Harper, 1951), pp. 190 ff.

CHAPTER 7: NON-CHRISTIAN RELIGIONS
AND THE STATE

1. *The New York Times* (May 18, 1964), p. 1.

2. Mircea Eliade, *The Sacred and the Profane: The Nature of Religion,* trans. Willard R. Trask (New York: Harper Torchbook, 1961), pp. 216-232.

3. Perhaps the most comprehensive single volume has been provided by John B. Noss, *Man's Religions* (3d ed., New York: Macmillan, 1963); a reliable account, available in a paperback edition, has been provided by Huston Smith, *The Religions of Man* (New York: Mentor Book, 1958).

4. G. van Der Leeuw, *Religion in Essence and Manifestation* (New York: Harper Torchbook, 1963), Vol. I, p. 266.

5. Joachim Wach, *Sociology of Religion* (Chicago: University of Chicago Press, 1944), pp. 54-108.

6. Joachim Wach, *Sociology of Religion* (Chicago: University of Chicago Press, 1944), pp. 109-204.

7. Joachim Wach, *Sociology of Religion* (Chicago: University of Chicago Press, 1944), pp. 144-145.

8. H. Richard Niebuhr, *Christ and Culture* (New York: Harper, 1951).

9. Interestingly, Huston Smith does not include a chapter on Shinto-ism in his book *The Religions of Man* (New York: Mentor Book, 1958).

10. Robert E. Hume, *The World's Living Religions: An Historical Sketch* (New York: Scribners, 1936), p. 83.

11. Joachim Wach, *Sociology of Religion* (Chicago: University of Chicago Press, 1944), p. 309.

12. Joachim Wach, *Sociology of Religion* (Chicago: University of Chicago Press, 1944), p. 307.

13. Morroe Berger, *The Arab World Today* (Garden City: Anchor Books, 1964), p. 274.

14. *Time* (Feb. 10, 1967), pp. 24-28.

15. Michael Novak, "Christianity: Renewed or Slowly Abandoned?," *Dædalus* (Winter, 1967), p. 263.

CHAPTER 8: THE CHURCH
AND TOTALITARIANISM

1. Sidney and Beatrice Webb, *The Truth About Soviet Russia* (New York: Longmans, Green, 1942).

2. Hannah Arendt, *The Origins of Totalitarianism* (New York: Harcourt, Brace, 1951), p. 9.

3. George F. Kennan, "Totalitarianism in the Modern World," *Totalitarianism*, ed. Carl J. Friedrich (New York: Grosset and Dunlap, 1964), p. 17.

4. Williston Walker, *A History of the Christian Church* (New York: Scribners, 1937), p. 320.

5. Yves M. J. Congar, *Lay People in the Church* (Westminster, Md.: Newman Press, 1957), p. 41.

6. Brian Tierney, *The Crisis of Church and State: 1050-1300* (Englewood Cliffs: Prentice-Hall, 1964).

7. A. D. Lindsay, *The Modern Democratic State* (New York: Oxford University Press, 1962), p. 156; a Roman Catholic, Luigi Sturzo, has described the long history of church-state relations from an official Roman Catholic viewpoint; see Luigi Sturzo, *Church and State*, 2 vols. (Notre Dame, Ind.: University of Notre Dame Press, 1962).

8. Hannah Arendt, *The Origins of Totalitarianism* (New York: Harcourt, Brace, 1951).

9. Carl J. Friedrich, "The Unique Character of Totalitarian Society," *Totalitarianism*, ed. Carl J. Friedrich (New York: Grosset and Dunlap, 1964), pp. 47-60.

10. George F. Kennan, "Totalitarianism in the Modern World," *Totalitarianism*, ed. Carl J. Friedrich (New York: Grosset and Dunlap, 1964), pp. 25-27.

11. *The Path to Dictatorship: 1918-1933, Ten Essays*, trans. from the German by John Conway (Garden City: Anchor Books, 1966).

12. George Orwell, *Nineteen Eighty-Four* (New York: Harcourt, Brace, 1949).

13. N. S. Timasheff, "Totalitarianism, Despotism, Dictatorship," *Totalitarianism*, ed. Carl J. Friedrich (New York: Grosset and Dunlap, 1964), pp. 39-46.

14. Erik H. Erikson, "Wholeness and Totality—A Psychiatric Contribution," *Totalitarianism*, ed. Carl J. Friedrich (New York: Grosset and Dunlap, 1964), pp. 156-171.

15. Else Frankel-Brunswik, "Environmental Controls and the Impoverishment of Thought," *Totalitarianism*, ed. Carl J. Friedrich (New York: Grosset and Dunlap, 1964), pp. 171-202.

16. Zbigniew K. Brzezinski, *Ideology and Power in Soviet Politics* (New York: Frederick A. Praeger, 1962), p. 19.

17. Carl J. Friedrich, "The Unique Character of Totalitarian Society," *Totalitarianism*, ed. Carl J. Friedrich (New York: Grosset and Dunlap, 1964), pp. 52-53.

18. Zbigniew K. Brzezinski, *Ideology and Power in Soviet Politics* (New York: Frederick A. Praeger, 1962), pp. 19-20.

19. Zbigniew K. Brzezinski, *Ideology and Power in Soviet Politics* (New York: Frederick A. Praeger, 1962), pp. 4-5.

20. Waldemar Gurian, "Totalitarianism as Political Religion," *Totalitarianism*, ed. Carl J. Friedrich (New York: Grosset and Dunlap, 1964), pp. 119-129.

21. Hannah Arendt, "Discussion," *Totalitarianism*, ed. Carl J. Friedrich (New York: Grosset and Dunlap, 1964), p. 134.

22. H. G. Wood, *Christianity and Communism* (New York: Roundtable Press, n.d.), p. 4.

23. *Basic Writings on Politics and Philosophy; Karl Marx and Friedrich Engels*, ed. Lewis S. Feuer (Garden City: Anchor Books, 1959), p. x.

24. Jerzy G. Gliksman, "Social Prophylaxis as a Form of Soviet Terror," *Totalitarianism*, ed. Carl J. Friedrich (New York: Grosset and Dunlap, 1964), p. 70.

25. Zbigniew K. Brzezinski, *Ideology and Power in Soviet Politics* (New York: Frederick A. Praeger, 1962), p. 48.

26. H. J. Muller, "Science Under Soviet Totalitarianism," *Totalitarianism*, ed. Carl J. Friedrich (New York: Grosset and Dunlap, 1964), p. 233.

27. Hans Kohn, *Political Ideologies of the Twentieth Century* (New York: Harper Torchbooks, 1966), pp. 57-58.

28. John Gunther, *Inside Russia Today* (New York: Harper, 1958), p. 147.

29. Editorial, "Church and State in Spain," *The New York Times* (June 13, 1966), p. 38.

30. Matthew Spinka, *The Church in Soviet Russia* (New York: Oxford University Press, 1956).

31. Matthew Spinka, *The Church in Soviet Russia* (New York: Oxford University Press, 1956), p. 68.

32. Max Ascoli and Arthur Feiler, *Fascism for Whom?* (New York: Norton, 1938), p. 274.

33. Franklin H. Littell, "The Protestant Churches and Totalitarianism (Germany 1933-45)," *Totalitarianism*, ed. Carl J. Friedrich (New York: Grosset and Dunlap, 1964), pp. 108-119.

34. "Johnson Invokes Spirit of Lincoln to End Race Bias," *The New York Times* (Feb. 13, 1967), pp. 1, 22.

35. Hannah Arendt, *The Origins of Totalitarianism* (New York: Harcourt, Brace, 1951), p. 157.

36. Winston S. Churchill, *The Aftermath* (New York: Scribners, 1929), p. 65.

37. Carmen Irizarry, *The Thirty Thousand: Modern Spain and Protestantism* (New York: Harcourt, Brace and World, 1966).

38. Peter H. Juviler and Henry W. Morton, eds., *Soviet Policy-Making: Studies of Communism in Transition* (New York: Frederick A. Praeger, 1967).

39. Frederick B. Pike, *The Conflict Between Church and State in Latin America* (New York: Knopf, 1964).

40. Karl W. Deutsch, "Cracks in the Monolith: Possibilities and Patterns of Disintegration in Totalitarian Systems," *Totalitarianism*, ed. Carl J. Friedrich (New York: Grosset and Dunlap, 1964), p. 332.

41. Elwin A. Smith, *Church and State in Your Community* (Philadelphia: Westminster Press, 1963); William Lee Miller, *The Protestant and Politics* (Philadelphia: Westminster Press, 1958).

CHAPTER 9: THE CHURCH
AND THE WELFARE STATE

1. Robert L. Heilbroner, *The Making of Economic Society* (Englewood Cliffs: Prentice-Hall, 1962), pp. 9-17.

2. *From Max Weber: Essays in Sociology*, trans., ed., and with an introduction by H. H. Gerth and C. Wright Mills (New York: Oxford University Press, 1946), pp. 59ff.; 294; 323ff.

3. William H. Beveridge, *Interdepartmental Committee Report on Social Insurance and Allied Services* (New York: Macmillan, 1942).

4. William H. Beveridge, *Full Employment in a Free Society* (New York: Norton, 1945).

5. *Ibid.*, p. 21.

6. Adam Smith, *The Wealth of the Nations* (New York: Modern Library, 1937).

7. John Kenneth Galbraith, *The Affluent Society* (Boston: Houghton Mifflin, 1958).

8. Niccolò Machiavelli, *The Prince* (New York: Modern Library, 1940), p. 56.

9. Niccolò Machiavelli, *Discourses*, trans. by Leslie Walker (New Haven: Yale University Press, 1950).

10. Thomas Hobbes, *Leviathan* (New York: Dutton, 1940).

11. Joseph A. Schumpeter, "The March into Socialism," *American Economic Review*, Vol. 40 (May, 1950), pp. 446-456.

12. Walter Lippmann, *The Good Society* (New York: Grosset and Dunlap, 1937).

13. John Dewey, "Authority and Social Change," in *John Dewey's Philosophy*, ed. by Joseph Ratner (New York: Random House, 1939).

14. Russell W. Davenport, "The Greatest Opportunity on Earth," *Fortune*, Vol. 40, No. 4 (Oct., 1949), p. 67.

15. Charles Merriam, *On the Agenda of Democracy* (Cambridge: Harvard University Press, 1941).

16. Arnold J. Toynbee, "Not the Age of Atoms but of Welfare for All," *The New York Times Magazine* (Oct. 21, 1951), pp. 15, 38.

17. John Stuart Mill, *On Liberty* (London: Longmans, 1926).

18. Alan Keith-Lucas, *The Church and Social Welfare* (Philadelphia: Westminster Press, 1962).

19. Haskell M. Miller, *Compassion and Community* (New York: Association Press, 1961), p. 126.

20. Commission on the Role of the Church in Social Welfare, *The Church in Social Welfare*: an Exploratory Study of the Role of the Lutheran Church in America in Social Welfare (New York: Board of Social Ministry, Lutheran Church in America, 1964), p. 65.

21. C. Stanley Lowell, *Separation and Religion* (Washington: Protestants and Other Americans United for Separation of Church and State, 1957).

22. Bernard J. Coughlin, *Church and State in Social Welfare* (New York: Columbia University Press, 1965), p. 32.

23. Dean M. Kelley, "Operational Consequences of Church-State Choices," *Social Progress: A Journal of Church and Society*, Vol. 57, No. 3 (Jan.-Feb., 1967), p. 18.

24. Bernard J. Coughlin, *Church and State in Social Welfare* (New York: Columbia University Press, 1965), p. 131.

CHAPTER 10: CHURCH AND STATE: THE DEVELOPING RELATIONSHIP

1. Daniel Bell, *End of Ideology* (Glencoe: Free Press, 1960).

2. Anson Phelps Stokes and Leo Pfeffer, *Church and State in the United States* (rev. 1-vol. ed., New York: Harper and Row, 1964), p. xi.

3. Franklin H. Littell, *From State Church to Pluralism: A Protestant Interpretation of Religion in American History* (Garden City: Anchor Books, 1962).

4. Robert F. Drinan, *Religion, The Court, and Public Policy* (New York: McGraw-Hill, 1963), p. 4.

5. Winthrop S. Hudson, *The Great Tradition of the American Churches* (New York: Harper, 1953), p. 172.

6. Will Herberg, *Catholic, Protestant, Jew; an Essay in American Religious Sociology* (Garden City: Doubleday, 1955).

7. *Relations Between Church and State* (Philadelphia: Office of the General Assembly, May, 1962), p. 7.

8. Emile Durkheim, *Division of Labor,* trans. George Simpson (Glencoe: Free Press, 1947).

9. Paul Tillich, *Theology of Culture,* ed. Robert C. Kimball (New York: Oxford University Press, 1959).

10. Gerhard Lenski, *The Religious Factor: A Sociological Study of Religion's Impact on Politics, Economics, and Family Life* (rev. ed., Garden City: Anchor Books, 1963).

11. Dietrich Bonhoeffer, *The Cost of Discipleship* (2d ed., New York: Macmillan, 1959), p. 235.

12. Winthrop S. Hudson, *The Great Tradition of the American Churches* (New York: Harper, 1953), p. 209.

13. Gibson Winter, *The Suburban Captivity of the Churches: An Analysis of Protestant Responsibility in the Expanding Metropolis* (New York: Macmillan, 1962); Peter Berger, *The Noise of Solemn Assemblies: Christian Commitment and the Religious Establishment in America* (Garden City: Doubleday, 1961).

14. Winthrop S. Hudson, *The Great Tradition of the American Churches* (New York: Harper, 1953), ch. 4.

15. Seymour Lipset, "The Value Patterns of Democracy: A Case Study in Comparative Analysis," *American Sociological Review*, Vol. 28, No. 4 (Aug., 1963), p. 529.

16. Dietrich Bonhoeffer, *The Cost of Discipleship* (2d ed., New York: Macmillan, 1959), pp. 235ff.

17. Karl Barth, *Community, State, and Church: Three Essays,* with an Introduction by Will Herberg (Garden City: Anchor Book, 1960), esp. pp. 26-27.

18. John C. Bennett, *Christians and the State* (New York: Scribners, 1958).

19. Evarts B. Greene, *Religion and the State: The Making and Testing of an American Tradition* (Indianapolis: National Foundation Press, 1947), p. 2.

20. *The New York Times* (July 17, 1966), p. 57.

21. Sam Duker, *The Public Schools and Religion: The Legal Context* (New York: Harper and Row, 1966).

22. Joseph Tussman, ed., *The Supreme Court on Church and State* (New York: Oxford University Press, 1962).

23. An earlier book of American law cases is John Joseph McGrath, *Church and State in American Law: Cases and Materials* (Milwaukee: Bruce, 1962).

24. Franklin H. Littell, "The Churches and the Body Politic," *Dædalus* (Winter, 1967), p. 40.

Index

NAMES

SUBJECTS